Rev L. P. Crockett

THE TEACHING MINISTRY
OF THE CHURCH

Books by James D. Smart
Published by The Westminster Press

The Teaching Ministry of the Church
The Recovery of Humanity
What a Man Can Believe
A Promise to Keep
Jesus, Stories for Children

In Collaboration with David Noel Freedman
God Has Spoken

The
TEACHING
MINISTRY
of the CHURCH

An Examination of the Basic Principles
of Christian Education

by
JAMES D. SMART

Philadelphia
THE WESTMINSTER PRESS

Library of Congress Catalog Card Number: 54-10569

To the memory of Walter W. Bryden,
late principal of Knox College, Toronto,
to whom a generation of Canadian students
are indebted for their awakening
to the importance of theology

CONTENTS

CONTENTS

FOREWORD

WHEN in 1944 I joined the staff of the Board of Christian Education of the Presbyterian Church in the U. S. A. to become editor in chief of a new curriculum development, I soon discovered that my first task was to think through the question of the theological foundations of the Church's educational program. In this task I should have been helpless if it had not been for the aid I received from Dr. Edward Paisley on many aspects of education; from Professor Leonard J. Trinterud, whose criticisms of my attempted formulations forced me more than once to begin the whole task afresh; and from Professor Hulda Niebuhr, who generously endured my questionings and put her wealth of knowledge in both education and theology at my disposal. Above all I am indebted to those who served with me on the editorial staff and shared the joy and pains of working out together not only the principles but also the intricate details of an educational program. So close was our relationship that I can no longer tell what is mine and what is theirs in my understanding of education. I must add, however, that none of these persons has read the present manuscript and none can be held responsible for any of the views expressed in it.

During my six years as an editor, nothing more than a sketch of basic principles could be attempted. Since returning to the pastorate in 1950 and since undertaking the duties of a lecturer in Christian education in 1951, I had been anxious to work out on a larger scale the implications of the viewpoint to which I had come. An invitation from the Presbyterian Theological Seminary in Austin, Texas, to give the Robert Jones Lectures in Christian Education at the midwinter conference of ministers, educators, and students, in February, 1953, propelled me into a preliminary draft of four of the chapters. During the winter of 1953–1954 these have been rewritten and expanded into the ten chapters of the present book. The interest shown at Austin in the content of the lectures greatly strengthened my sense of the urgency of proceeding to publication.

I have made it my aim to consider, not the theological bases of Presbyterian education, but rather the theological bases of Christian education in the most comprehensive sense. For that reason I have taken the doctrine of the Trinity, to which all Christian Churches, Protestant and Roman Catholic, give adherence, as my essential starting point, and have tried simply to show the character of the educational program that results when that doctrine is allowed to have its full force in our thinking and in our practices. It is my hope therefore that this book may have significance in forwarding a more ecumenical approach to the problems of Christian education.

Finally, I must acknowledge my debt to my own family: to my wife, whose understanding of children has been a constant influence in all my thinking; and to my three daughters, who, as they have moved up through the departments of the church school, have provided me with firsthand information about what goes on in the minds of children and young people of various ages.

JAMES D. SMART

1

THE TEACHING FUNCTION OF THE CHURCH

THE existence of Christian education as a distinct area of study and action in the Church rests upon the assumption that the Church of Jesus Christ has, of necessity, a teaching function. The Church must teach, just as it must preach, or it will not be the Church. Responsibility for teaching rests upon the whole church even though only certain members undertake specific teaching assignments, just as responsibility for the maintenance of the pure preaching of the gospel and the right observance of the sacraments rests upon the whole church, even though only a limited number of persons are called upon to preach or to dispense the sacraments. Teaching belongs to the essence of the Church and a church that neglects this function of teaching has lost something that is indispensable to its nature as a church. It is a defective church if it is lacking at this point, just as a church in which the gospel ceases to be preached in its purity or a church in which the sacraments cease to be rightly administered is a defective church.

THE CONFUSION ABOUT THE STATUS OF EDUCATION

Strange as it may seem, this foundation principle of Christian education remains largely unrecognized today, and, strangest of all, unrecognized often by those who are devoting their lives to the work of teaching in the Church. The religious education movement of the past half century has often tended to feel itself more closely related to secular education than to the Church. In some of its representatives there has even been a questioning whether it should remain in direct continuity with the historic Christian Church. They have found a Church too narrow that lets itself be bound and limited in any way by a Biblical revelation, and they have called not only for a recognition of the revelations of all religions but also for an experimental approach by which the educator may expect to attain religious developments beyond anything to be found in the Christian or any other religion. It is little wonder that education based upon these convictions should sit very loosely in relation to the Church and should be uninterested in exploring the Biblical evidence for the rootage of teaching in the nature of the Church. It is much happier to have its roots in modern secular education rather than in any tradition of the Church. Even where the educator stands determinedly in the Christian tradition, the interest has been much more emphatic in exploring the educational aspects of the field than in following up the Christian, or distinctly theological, aspects. The literature of Christian education is marked by the absence of serious and thorough theological investigations. The Christian educator apparently has in general assumed that his subject is educational rather than theological.

This assumption has had serious consequences for the entire range of developments in the Church's educational program. Schools for training educational directors have been strong in educational subjects but weak in Biblical and theological subjects. Programs for the training of church school teachers have been specific and effective on all questions of methodology but singularly vague and ineffective when forced to deal with theological questions concerning the nature of the gospel and of the Church. Most churches have consequently been reluctant to recognize trained religious educators as ministers of the Church, and uncertainty and uneasiness have persisted in wide sections of the Church about the whole modern development of religious education.

In quite another quarter the failure to recognize the necessity of the teaching function to the Church has resulted in a misconception of the ministry. Very widely the task of the minister is conceived as primarily that of a preacher and pastor. If he carries any educational responsibility, that is something added which does not properly belong to his office. He does it only because his church cannot afford an educational director or because he cannot find laymen who will accept the full responsibility. He escapes from it at the earliest opportunity that he may concentrate upon what he considers his essential functions. Under heavy pressure, if any duty has to be dropped or left with scant attention, it is the educational one. When asked why they do not have classes for the training of teachers, ministers invariably answer that there is no time for them. They would not excuse themselves from preaching or from administering the sacraments or from any of the other essential functions of their ministry with a plea of " no time." Yet here they do so without any qualms, for to them the educational function is not essential to their ministry. Many theological seminaries in their curriculums mirror this defective conception of the ministry. They are organized for the training of a ministry that will be almost exclusively homiletic and pastoral and in which education is not expected to have much place.

It is clear, then, that there exists a very real uncertainty about the place of education and the educator in the Church. The educator himself is uncertain about where he belongs both in relationship to the Church and in relationship to the theological curriculum. The Church is uncertain, and in most of its branches has not been able to make up its mind, whether or not a Christian educator belongs in the full ministry of the Church. The theological seminary is uncertain about the character of the training that should be given, on the one hand, to those who are to be ministers, and, on the other hand, to those who are to be directors of education. Surely such wide uncertainty indicates the need for an investigation of the rootage of education in the Church.

PREACHING AND TEACHING IN THE OLD TESTAMENT

In Old Testament times the prophet, the ancestor in Israel of the Christian preacher, is so predominant that the entire work of teaching falls into the shadow. But it was very definitely there, and the persistence of a holy faith in Israel from generation to generation was the consequence, not of the prophet's preaching alone, but also of faithful teaching by unnumbered and unremembered Israelites. The book of Deuteronomy, though it originated not long before the Exile, bears witness to an emphasis upon teaching that undoubtedly reaches far back in the history of Israel. According to Deut., ch. 6, the response of the Israelites to God's love for them as his people and to his deliverance of them was to be, first of all, a love for him that would encompass their entire being, and then, as an expression of this love for God, a teaching of the faith that was now theirs to their children and to their grandchildren. The love for God and the activity of teaching are inseparable. The life that Israel had with God as a community in covenant with him, sustained by faith in him and governed in all its life by his will as expressed in the Commandments, must be communicated to the rising generations. This education was not to be merely a transmission of laws and ideas, but rather an extending of the covenant relationship ever more widely, drawing each new Israelite into its privileges and responsibilities. For an Israelite to fail at this point and so let his descendants be deprived of their only true life in covenant with God would be an indication that he did not love God with all his heart and mind and soul. The entire adult community carried this responsibility; if they were faithful Israelites, they would teach the faith to which they were committed, telling the story of God's dealings with his people in the past and making plain what he expected of them and offered to them in the present.

It is noteworthy that, in this sixth chapter of Deuteronomy, emphasis is laid upon the importance of persistence in teaching and upon the utilization of informal opportunities. There were to be regular ceremonies in the homes, which would naturally become the occasion of religious instruction, with the father acting as priest and teacher. This ministry of the father in the family eventually became so deeply rooted that it has persisted in Judaism to the present day. But such formal occasions were not sufficient. So important was the communication of faith from one generation to the other that the Israelite was exhorted to converse on the subject not only when sitting at home but when walking on the road, not only at the beginning of each day but also at its close, and to have symbols fastened on his body and on the gates of his house that would remind his family constantly of God's word of commandment.

In the book of The Proverbs we learn that both father and mother in Israel were included in this ministry of faith. " My son, hear the instruction of thy father, and forsake not the law of thy mother " (Prov. 1:8). Undoubtedly it is because the teaching function was discharged so largely in the home that we hear so little about it elsewhere in the Old Testament. Of its effectiveness the best witness is the history of Israel's faith, for it was out of these homes that the prophets came. Men marvel that a farmer such as Amos, growing up in the rough country on the edge of the Judean hills, with few cultural advantages, should suddenly step forth as a prophet of God, whose barbed messages were expressed in a poetic form of superb quality. How came this farmer to have such insight into the history and the destiny of his people and to possess such mastery of literary expression? He was an educated man, behind whom lay centuries of life and thought in Israel, and, when he spoke, the whole of Israel's heritage was embodied in his words. By what human means was that heritage transmitted to him? We have no definite evidence, but the greatest likelihood is that he was the product of one of those homes in which parents, grandparents, and great-grandparents had faithfully discharged their teaching function.

It is sufficient for our purposes if it has now been made plain that the word by which Israel had its life as the covenant people of God required *not just one but two* services; it required *prophets* who would proclaim it ever afresh, calling the nation, in so far as it had fallen away into unbelief, to repent and return to God; and it required *teachers* in every home and in every street who would not rest until they saw a living faith in their children and in their neighbors. That Israelites were to teach not only the members of their own families but others whom they could reach is apparent from Jeremiah's description of the days of the new covenant, when " they shall teach no more every man his neighbor, and every man his brother, saying, Know the Lord: for they shall all know me." This responsibility for teaching rested upon every Israelite.

The prophet himself seems to have been both preacher and teacher. It is impossible to conceive of an Isaiah or a Jeremiah contenting himself with saying no more concerning God and his purpose with Israel than what could be expressed in those public utterances to the nation as a whole which are preserved in the collections of their prophecies. We have in their books only fragments of all that they had to say in their lifetime. From a prophet of such stature as Nathan we have only a single dramatic incident, preserved because of its importance in the history of David. But here and there we find hints that groups of disciples gathered about the great prophets. Only once are they mentioned by Isaiah (ch. 8:16). Jeremiah had his disciple and scribe, Baruch, and may well have had others who were not satisfied to hear him only on public occasions. Second Isaiah, with his warm personal message of encouragement to faith, drew about him a circle of believers. They appear at a number of points in his writings. He distinguished them sharply from the unbelievers (chs. 50:10, 11; 57:1–3), and addressed them as " ye that tremble at his [God's] word " (ch. 66:5). In circles of disciples such as this, the prophets exercised a teaching function. We see it quite distinctly with John the Baptist, who preached to the crowds but taught his disciples. Thus, even in the prophet, alongside the work of preaching stands the work of teaching, both of them services required of the prophet by the word of God which he served.

In the post-exilic period, as the prophet fell into the shadow, the scribe came forward to take his place. The disaster of the final destruction of Jerusalem and the scattering of the nation in exile set the stamp of validity upon the words of the great pre-exilic prophets and gave to their collected writings an impressive authority. In the Law and the Prophets the nation now possessed an authoritative word of God in written form. The exposition of these writings became increasingly important, and the scribe as their expositor commanded the central place. Perhaps the rapid decline of living prophecy was inevitable, the assumption being now so widely made that the word of God in the Scriptures was henceforward to the nation what the prophet had once been. Teaching thus displaced preaching and became primary. The scribe was a teacher. In Ezra we see, not a preacher, but a teacher at work in the congregation (Neh. 8:1–8) with the Scriptures open before him, reading them distinctly and interpreting them to the people (v. 8).

The history of Judaism from this point serves as a warning how serious an error it is to let the living proclamation of the word of God be displaced as the primary service which God's people must render to it, and how dangerous it is to let teaching stand alone. The expectation that God should speak his word in the present moment is likely then to die away. Revelation is regarded as belonging en-

tirely to the past, and the duty of the believer in the present is to reg-
ulate his life according to what has been revealed concerning the will
of God in the past. Out of this order of things could come only a
legalism such as developed in Judaism. Faith is then loyalty to the
tradition as set down once and for all in the Scriptures. Judaism
could have been saved from its legalism only by the persistence of
the prophet alongside the scribe. The teaching of the scribes could
not have become a closed system if the prophet's voice had still
sounded into the life of the nation; and when the Old Testament
prophet came alive again in John the Baptist and Jesus, the closed
system of the scribes was shattered. Legalisms ancient and modern
cannot abide the voice of the prophet.

It is a very serious matter, then, to reverse the earlier order and to
let the teaching ministry take precedence over and even displace entirely the prophetic or preaching ministry. This has at times happened in the modern church. We dare not let our enthusiasm for
education or our conviction of the importance of the teaching function in the Church lead us into excesses in which we disparage the
importance of preaching and are in danger of falling into errors
similar to those of post-exilic Judaism.

Preaching and Teaching in the New Testament

In the ministry of Jesus it is an impossibility to draw a sharp line
of distinction between preaching and teaching. This does not mean
that preaching and teaching are just two names for the same function. There is preaching and there is teaching, and, as we shall see,
there is a very important difference between them. Yet they are so
intermingled that the one cannot be totally separated from the other.
To the crowds who thronged about Jesus he was more the teacher
than the prophet. "Teacher" or "rabbi" was their commonest title
for him, even though his teaching had in it an authority and power
that set it sharply apart from that of the rabbis. Their impression of
him set him definitely in the category of rabbis or teachers (Mark
1:22). This fact stands out even more clearly when we recollect that
no one thought of classifying John the Baptist as anything other
than a prophet. It is inconceivable that anyone should have called
him "Rabbi." Yet they called Jesus "Rabbi"! Nicodemus (John

3:2) said, "Thou art a teacher sent from God," and not, "Thou art a prophet sent from God." The prophetic character was sufficiently plain in Jesus to make some people think he might be John the Baptist, or Elijah, or Jeremiah come back from the dead, and he most certainly thought of himself as belonging in line, not with the rabbis, but with the prophets. Nevertheless teaching occupied so large a place alongside preaching in his ministry that the impression of the "Great Teacher" was created and still remains. Mark describes him constantly as teaching (Mark 4:1, 2; 6:2, 6; 8:31; 9:31; 12:35). The command of the risen Christ to his disciples that they should carry the gospel into all the world has in Mark the word "preach" but in Matthew the word "teach." Acts 1:1 speaks of the Gospel of Luke as containing the record of "all that Jesus began to do and teach." And of the apostles it is said, in Acts 5:42, "They ceased not to teach and preach Jesus Christ." The apostles were not only preachers but also teachers and it was the same gospel that they both preached and taught.

Paul leaves no doubt in our minds that he considered the preaching of Christ and him crucified as his primary responsibility, and yet he is constantly pictured as both preaching and teaching. In Ephesus he taught in the Greek disputation style in the school of Tyrannus. In his letters to Timothy he lays very great weight upon the importance of teaching, both in Timothy's own ministry and in the Church in general. For this work of teaching a special order in the ministry is recognized alongside apostles, prophets, evangelists, and pastors. In I Cor. 12:28, Paul places teachers next in order after prophets, but in Eph. 4:11, evangelists and pastors are placed ahead of them. The two passages, however, make it plain that teachers were an essential part of the church's ministry. All ministers had a responsibility for teaching, but a specific responsibility, most likely that of training converts, was assigned to these teachers.

We can understand the importance that was set upon teaching in the Early Church, and the urgency of it, when we consider the large numbers who in response to the gospel were asking to be received into the Church. Whether they had a Jewish or a Gentile background, they required a period of instruction and rethinking if they were actually to leave behind their old world and become in any full sense sharers in the Kingdom of Christ. The thoroughness with which this work of re-education was done would determine largely whether or not the new converts became effective Christian disciples. It was not sufficient for a man to repent and believe; he had to be led on step by step until he so understood his new faith that he could bear convincing witness to it in his daily walk of life. His guide in this period of training was the teacher.

We may sum up the entire consideration by saying that, in both Old and New Testaments, the word of God in which God reveals himself and in revealing himself comes to man for his salvation, requires two services primarily of those who respond to it: first, that they should preach this word that has come to them, and secondly, that they should teach it. The omission of either service is unfaithfulness to God. There must be preaching and there must be teaching.

The Distinction Between Preaching and Teaching

We must try now to see why this ministry of the word is twofold. Why must there be preaching *and* teaching? Why is not one sufficient? The fact of a difference between the two is evident wherever we look. In the Old Testament, what the prophet does as a preacher of the word is something different from what he or any other adult in Israel does as teacher, yet not so different as to destroy the unity between the two. In the New Testament, one word is not sufficient to describe either the ministry of Jesus or the ministry of the apostles. They are both preachers and teachers. So also in the present-day church. Preaching is preaching and teaching is teaching, and yet good preaching is also teaching and good teaching has in it the note of the preacher's proclamation. Wherein are they together, and wherein are they different?

They are together in being both the service of the Word of God. It is the same Jesus Christ who is to be taught and who is to be preached. The content of preaching and of teaching is the same. But preaching essentially is the proclamation of this Word of God *to man in his unbelief*. Both outside and inside the Church that definition proves adequate. Preaching is the call to men in their sin and unbelief to repent and receive the good news that God is ready to come to them, and that, by the power of his Word and his Spirit dwelling in them, he will establish them in the glad free life of his Kingdom. We need the preaching of the word as Christians, because, no matter how far we have gone in faith, there still remains a root of sin and unbelief in us, a place in each of us into which the humbling, transforming word of the gospel has not yet come. The preacher who makes the mistake of thinking that the good Christians sitting in the pews before him no longer need to hear the call to repentance or the proclamation of the nearness of the Kingdom in Christ has lost all understanding both of the gospel itself and of the natures of those to whom he is commissioned to proclaim it. Preaching addresses itself always to man in the distress of his separation from and rebellion against God.

What, then, is teaching? Teaching essentially (but not exclusively) addresses itself to the situation of the man who has repented and turned to God and to the situation of children of believers who through the influence of their parents have in them a measure of faith, even though they have also in them a large measure of unbelief. There have been Christian sects that have set such an exclusive emphasis upon repentance and faith that they have abandoned the work of teaching. Children, before conversion, were regarded as so completely unbelievers that they were incapable of understanding anything of Christian truth. All attempts to instruct them would necessarily be wasted. And when they or others were converted, they were immediately, by God's converting act, transplanted into a state of grace in which instruction was superfluous. Such an order and such a viewpoint are un-Biblical. God has established a function of teaching in his Church as well as a function of preaching, that his work of grace may take place, not just at one decisive moment in a man's life, but throughout the whole of it, if possible from earliest infancy until the most advanced years. God's word must come to men, not just in one way, although that one way of prophetic proclamation is indispensable, but in many ways, and through every possible channel, that no opportunity may be lost for claiming the whole of life for God.

While this is the essential concern of teaching in the Church, the growth in grace of the believer, it may also prove an effective approach to unbelievers. Paul, in the School of Tyrannus at Ephesus, was undoubtedly doing the work of an evangelist among unbelievers, and yet he is described as teaching, and, indeed, using the Greek teaching method of public disputation. Both Paul and Jesus taught in the synagogues, most likely using familiar rabbinical methods in reaching the minds of their hearers. Here, the term " teaching " seems to refer to the informal rabbinic character of the approach in contrast to the more formal prophetic act of preaching. What is being done, however, is indistinguishable from what is done in preaching. The endeavor at every point is to gain a hearing for the good news that in Jesus Christ the time is fulfilled, the Kingdom is at hand, so that every man may repent and believe.

Much harm has been done to a right understanding of the place of teaching in the church by the wide acceptance of the views of C. H. Dodd on *kerygma* and *didache* (the original New Testament preaching and teaching) as enunciated in his *Apostolic Preaching and Its Developments,* published in 1936. " The New Testament writers," he says, " draw a clear distinction between preaching and teaching. The distinction is preserved alike in Gospels, Acts, Epistles, and Apocalypse, and must be considered characteristic of early Christian usage in general. Teaching (*didaskein*) is in a large majority of cases ethical instruction. Occasionally it seems to include what we should call apologetic, that is, the reasoned commendation of Christianity to persons interested, but not yet convinced. Sometimes, especially in the Johannine writings, it includes the exposition of theological doctrine. Preaching, on the other hand, is the public proclamation of Christianity to the non-Christian world." Perhaps the reason this statement has won such unquestioning acceptance has been because teaching as we know it in the present-day Church has been so largely ethical instruction, and because preachers have so often thought they were exercising a teaching ministry when they confined themselves in their sermons to ethical instruction.

As a protest against the insipid moralism of a pulpit that has forgotten the kerygma that was the indispensable essence of the Church's original preaching, Dodd's statement has performed a valuable service. But in alleging that in the Biblical period teaching was confined largely to ethical instruction, he has validated what is actually one of the chief sicknesses of education in the Church, that it has been so consistently moralistic in its character and has lacked the depth and power of the kerygma. He has done nothing less than detach the work of teaching from all essential relation to the kerygma. In this, as we have already seen, Dodd is out of line with the entire Biblical tradition. He has differentiated between preaching and teaching in a way in which the Old Testament and the New Testament consistently refuse to do. Upon his interpretation, they cease to have a single content and to parallel services which the Church renders to one and the same word of God. Acts 5:42 would need to be rewritten then to say that the apostles " preached Jesus Christ and taught Christian ethics," instead of what is written: " They ceased not to teach and preach Jesus Christ."

The distinction between preaching and teaching must be maintained, but it must not be allowed to become a false and un-Biblical distinction. When the Church exalts teaching at the expense of preaching, it inevitably becomes moralistic and legalistic. This can be seen in rabbinic Judaism and also in wide areas of present-day Protestantism. People are assumed to need only teaching. The rock of unbelief and sin in them is forgotten. A gospel that calls men to repent and believe, sending them down into the death of their old self in repentance that they may rise into the new life of faith, seems out of place. Salvation becomes a quite simple matter of having the right ideals and measuring up to them as well as we can. Teaching, without a kerygmatic preaching alongside it to remind it of the common origin and common task of both, can very easily become a total falsification of Christianity.

Equally unfortunate are the results when the ministry confines its attention to the kerygma, the proclamation of the gospel, and ignores the task of teaching. Such a ministry fails because it refuses to follow the Word that is preached into the lives of the hearers and to take seriously the problems that the believer begins at once to meet in his response to the gospel and in his personal growth in the knowledge of God. The ministry thus becomes an oracular function in which the preacher's only responsibility is to declare the Word of God in sermons. He withholds himself from that more intimate contact with his people in which he might learn more accurately the character of the seed he has been sowing in their lives, by seeing what grows from it. He keeps at a distance from the minds of his people. No man knows rightly what he himself has said until he examines what men have heard from him and sees what consequences follow in practical life. The minister who refuses to come down from his pulpit and participate in the work of teaching is like a farmer who scatters seed on the land and refuses to do anything more until the harvest. In fact, if he withholds himself from the more open and vulnerable situation of the teacher, he is likely to lack that intimate knowledge of what is happening in his people's lives which alone makes it possible for him to be an effective harvester. The ministry of the Word is a ministry to people, not in the mass but as individuals, to be exercised with loving care. The work of sowing is only partly done in sermons. It needs also to be done in smaller groups and from house to house. But in these situations it takes the form of teaching. So also the work of harvesting may be done in pulpit or classroom, in the home or on the street. Both preacher and teacher must be watching for the time of harvest when the grain is ripe and a new stage of development ready to begin. Preaching and teaching are both essential to a full ministry, and the lack of either one renders it defective. The implications of this principle we must leave to the following chapters.

2

EDUCATION AND THEOLOGY

THERE has been, and still is, a great vagueness about where education belongs in the field of theology. There have been educators who have denied that it has anything to do with theology, and have bitterly resented the raising of theological questions in the educational realm, as though they were out of place there. On the other hand, there have been theologians who have regarded Christian education as nothing more than a study of educational psychology and techniques and have withheld from it recognition as an essential theological discipline. Professors of Christian education in theological seminaries have often felt this uncertainty concerning their status, as though they were interlopers in the school of theology, admitted not because the theological curriculum would be incomplete without them but because of a practical demand from the Church for ministers with some measure of educational competence. Again, there is the attitude, with which Paul Tillich, in his Dogmatics I (page 32), finds himself in agreement, which regards not only Christian education but all the practical departments of the theological curriculum as mere studies of practical techniques, and so essentially outside the scope of theology proper, nothing more than methodological addenda to the curriculum.

THE WORD AND THE CHURCH

It is impossible to understand the relation of education to theology until first we have defined the function of theology itself. And since theology is a function of the Church, our conception of it will be determined by our conception of the Church. The Church is the human instrument called into being by God's revelation of himself

24

in his Word, a people of God living in response to him as his witnesses in the world, that through them God may be known ever more widely as he has been known to them. The revelation of God creates the Church. Apart from the revelation, it has no real existence. It is not a self-existent reality, but comes into being and remains in being only as God makes himself known in his Word. The revelation itself demands a human channel of communication. God's revelation of himself is not a communication merely of information about himself or of abstract truths which can be conveyed in words alone or trusted wholly to the pages of a book. It is God himself who is revealed — not just something about God but a truth that is at the same time a life, a personal life, and if it is to be communicated to the world, it must be through persons in whom the life as well as the truth can be embodied. God reveals himself to persons that through them he may become known to yet other persons, and the Church is the fellowship of those persons to whom and through whom God is making himself known.

The Scriptures are the record preserved by the Church of how God revealed himself to it and so called it into being, also of how, by continuing to reveal himself to it, he sustained it in being. It is the record of the Word of God that created the Church, and that is able to create the Church ever afresh when it is rightly heard and obeyed. Thus the Word of God and the Church are inseparable. Both are necessary to God that he may reveal himself in judgment and in mercy as the God that he is. Word and Church belong together, and in no other order than that — the Word first and the Church second. The Word creates the Church, not the Church the Word. The Church is wholly dependent upon the Word, and has no existence without it. The Word without the Church remains still the Word of God, merely bereft for the time of the means of communicating itself to the world. And it does not remain long bereft. Where one Church fails in its ministry, the Word of God is able to call into being another Church for its service. It has happened more than once.

Israel traced its origin as a people of God to Abraham. That which set Abraham and his family apart from all other Mesopotamians, and gave them a unique destiny, was a revelation of God to Abraham, and through him to his family. It was the uniqueness of Abraham's knowledge of God that accounted for the uniqueness of his destiny. He was conscious of himself and his family as being marked out to be witnesses of God. God needed a man through whom he might reveal himself to men, and he chose Abraham. Why he chose this one man from Ur of the Chaldees and not some other, we cannot know, any more than we can know why he chose Isaiah or Jeremiah or Jesus of Nazareth, or Paul or Martin Luther or ourselves. We cannot penetrate the mystery of God's election and explain why he chose one and not another. Rather, we have to start from the fact of God's choosing, that a revelation, which was meant for all men, had to begin with someone, in order through that one eventually to reach all. The witness of Scripture is that it began with Abraham. God, in order that he might reveal himself to mankind, called a man and a family into his service.

The creative power of the revelation appears even more spectacularly in the story of the Exodus. God's revelation of himself to Moses resulted in the creation of Israel, the covenant people of God, out of a disorganized band of slaves. A nation came into being, with the conviction that it had a special destiny in the world so indelibly stamped upon it that nothing during three thousand years or more was able to erase it. Unfortunately, often the nation in later years retained the sense of destiny but lost sight of the origin and true meaning of its special relationship to God. The Israelites forgot that they were chosen as a people in whose midst God might make himself known, so that through them he might one day be acknowledged as Lord of the entire creation.

In the New Testament, the Word spoken by Jesus Christ and incarnate in him called a new people of God into being. The concentrated effort of Jesus in his lifetime, and of his apostles after his death, was to win Israel to the service of the gospel and to a recognition of it as the fulfillment or completion of God's revelation of himself in Israel. The first Christians were most reluctant, even after the crucifixion of Jesus, to break with the old Israel, and did so only when they were driven out of the synagogues by their compatriots' rejection of them and their gospel. A Church long prepared for the service of this revelation refused to submit itself to the re-creating power of the revelation. The Jewish Church rejected the word and thereby destroyed its own validity as a Church. But the word of the gospel then proved its power to call a new Church into being. Out of every nation of the ancient world men responded to it, and there was shortly to be seen a Universal Church, more powerful by far than anything men had ever dreamed of before.

The priority of the Word of revelation to the Church is called into question by the Roman Catholic and Anglo-Catholic theories of the Church. They reverse the order, giving to the Church the primary place and making the Word of revelation secondary to, and dependent upon, the Church. In support of this, they point to the fact that the Church has always preceded the Scriptures; that in history the order has been first the Church and then the Scriptures written by the Church. On this basis they assert that the authority of the Church is primary, and that it is for the Church, as God's chosen representative in the world, to say what the revelation of God is. This theory reaches its most extreme form in the doctrine of the infallibility of the pope, and in those encyclicals in which the pope claims for his word an authority as truth that dare not be questioned, even though it be without foundation in Scripture or in direct contradiction to what is found in Scripture. The Church is then the controller of the revelation. The error in this doctrine is not obscure. It is true that, in both Old and New Testaments, there is a Church before there are any Scriptures and that the Church creates the Scriptures, but these Scriptures in both Testaments are set down as the record of the revelation that brought the Church into existence. The invariable testimony of the Church is not that it determined but that it was determined by the Word that it heard from God. The Biblical order is always: first the word of revelation, then the Church, and then the record of the revelation in the Church.

There has been a corresponding Protestant error in which the Word of the Scriptures has been cut apart from the Church and made to stand alone, as though a Church were not really necessary to the revelation. "The Bible and the Bible alone is the Word of God. God's chosen means of revealing himself is through the texts of Scripture. The Church serves a useful purpose only in so far as it acquaints people with the Scriptures, but that is all." Thus, in church school the studies are often limited to the Bible alone and nothing is taught concerning the Church or its history. Logically in line with this is an ignoring of the fallibility of the human Church of Old and New Testament times which brought the Scriptures into be- ing, and an interpreting of the Scriptures as though they had come directly from the mouth of God, rather than through the instrumen- tality of a very human Church of God. The most apt way of an- swering this error is to point to the fact that our Lord committed his revelation, not to a book, but to persons. There was a deep reason for that. Jesus was not willing to set down his gospel in a book be- cause, by its nature as a truth which is also life, the very life of God himself being given to man, the gospel had to be embodied in per- sons, and witness had to be borne to it by persons, if it was to be heard and understood. Jesus entrusted his gospel to a Church, and the New Testament Scriptures were set down, not as a substitute for the Church, but in order to keep the Church true and ever awake to the gospel that had been entrusted to it. The Church is the neces- sary instrument of the revelation, but it is wholly dependent upon the revelation, being called into life by it and being sustained in life only as the revelation sounds in and through it ever afresh.

The Church's Response to the Word

The Church, as we have seen, lives in response to the Word of God. It is the human partner in a covenant in which the other part- ner is the unseen God. The covenant is created and maintained from God's side by his revealing himself constantly in his Word, so that he can be known as the God that he is, and from man's side by a response of his whole being that begins in thanksgiving and praise, continues in his offering himself for the service of God, and is completed by an obedience that takes in all things in life.

We may distinguish different elements in the Church's response to God, all of them necessary to the whole; in fact, the loss of any one, or the deformity of any one, threatens the entire Church with death, just as sickness in any member of the human body is a sick- ness of the entire body, setting its life in danger.

Before all else, the Church responds to God in worship. God's giving of himself to us in his Word calls forth from us a giving of our whole selves to him. The action of worship is double: God comes to us in his Word and we come to him in thanksgiving, confession, praise, and dedication. We cannot come to him except he first come to us. Our coming is wholly response and is possible only as the same God who speaks to us in his Word takes possession of our hearts by the power of his Spirit and moves us to yield ourselves to him. Worship must therefore be so ordered that it provides abundant opportunity both for God's coming to us in his Word and Spirit, and for our response to him. Where such worship takes place, God is no longer distant but is present, and not just with his people, but *in* his people. They are a people who, in their response to God, have come to be indwelt by God. They are now the two or three who, meeting together in the name of Jesus Christ, have the promise fulfilled that he himself will be in the midst of them, i.e., *in* them, making them a human body for himself in which he may dwell and through which he may speak and act.

A second element in the Church's response to God is its ministry of the Word. This cannot be separated from worship, for without it worship has lost its center, and yet it must be considered apart. God's Word, wherever it is rightly heard, calls for those who hear it to offer themselves as witnesses through whom it may be heard by others. The ministry of the Word therefore belongs in the nature of things to every true believer. The riches of mercy and understanding and love that we receive from God in the gospel put us so far in debt to him that nothing we can ever do can discharge the obligation. Like Paul, we owe a debt to all men to share with them what God in his goodness has given to us. Thus the Church, in its very nature, exists to serve the Word which is the source of its life. The Christian who withholds himself from this service of the Word, who thinks that he can be a Christian without being a witness, actually is refusing to be the Church for which God calls in his Word. A congregation of people who renounce this service of the Word, who fail to fit themselves for its intelligent discharge, and consider worship, financial contributions, and reasonably moral living an adequate response to God and discharge of their debt to him, have become something other than a Christian Church.

In addition to this ministry of the Word which belongs to every member of the Church, there exist special ministeries, those of preaching and teaching. God has ever commanded that his Word be preached and that it be taught. For these ministries the Church must choose out fit persons in whom it finds evidence of special gifts for preaching and teaching. The gifts are from God. The Church must in every age be confident that God has endowed men and women with such gifts in sufficient numbers to meet the need, but the Church itself has the task of recognizing where such gifts are present and calling them into service, providing at the same time opportunity for their development by training.

In recent years, many Protestant churches have failed to take their proper responsibility in recognizing the gifts of the ministry and in calling those who possess such gifts into the Church's service. The idea has become widespread that one must wait for individuals to have some unusual spiritual experience that may be interpreted as a call from God. A variation of this idea is that no one should be sent to the foreign field who does not have within himself a clearly defined call, not just to the ministry, but to the foreign field. Therefore, mission boards, instead of seeking out persons who clearly have gifts from God that fit them for foreign service, and then in the name of Christ calling them to this service, wait for individuals to appear who in some way or other have themselves arrived at the conviction that they have such gifts and should go to the foreign field. The missions, and also the ministry of the Church, have suffered severely because of the failure of the Church to take seriously the fact that, while the gifts of the ministry are from God, the recognition of them and the call to those who possess them to use them in the service of God are acts that God expects of his Church. Perhaps if a larger number within the Church knew themselves called to the ministry of the Word that belongs to *all* believers, the Church's task of recognizing the special gifts of preaching and teaching would not be so difficult as it is and the call to these special ministries would not be allowed to remain so purely individual a matter.

A third aspect of the Church's response to God, alongside its worship and its service of the Word, is its obedience to the Word of God in the entirety of life. All its worship becomes empty and vain, no matter how right it is in form; all its preaching and teaching become mere words, glancing off the hard surface of life, unless there is a response of obedience to God in the concrete situations of daily life. We do right to call our worship a service and preaching and teaching twin services of God, but for their validation they require this other, more difficult, service of God in the entire conduct of life — personal, social, economic, political. The prophets, by their blunt repudiation of religion in which a beautiful ritual and a correct doctrine existed without any corresponding concern about what was happening in the market place or in the homes or the palaces of Israel, have made it very clear that no response is acceptable to God that does not take in the whole of life. The God of the prophets is not interested merely in a so-called " spiritual " aspect of life, but claims for himself an absolute sovereignty, first over the whole of Israel's life, and then over the whole of the world's life. So also in the New Testament Jesus Christ lays claim to a Lordship, not over the inner unseen part of man's being alone, but over man's total being. The apostles were not content to proclaim him King and Head of the Church and Lord of the souls of men, but called him King of Kings and Lord of Lords, and recognized no line beyond which his sovereignty should not run.

It was this totalitarian claim of Jesus himself, and later, on his behalf, by his apostles, that made the gospel so difficult to accept. The rich young ruler was not the only man who was saddened by the discovery that Jesus would not recognize a conditional loyalty as genuine faith, but demanded of a man an unconditional faith in which no part of his being was held back from submission to the rule of the Kingdom. Faith must be total or it is not faith. The Church's service of God, therefore, does not end when congregations have conducted their services of worship and have provided for the preaching and teaching of the Word of God. Rather, it has only made a beginning and the test of all that happens in worship, preaching, and teaching is what now begins to happen in the homes, in the places of business, in the schools of the community, on the streets, in the factories, in the institutions of government, and, even farther than that, in the literature and music which mirror the deeper life of the community.

The Task of Theology

The Church exists in hearing and responding to God as he comes to it in his Word. Any failure or perversion either in its hearing of the Word or in any part of its response is the Church's death. But, because we, who are in the Church, are blind and sinful human creatures and have a residue of blindness and sin and unbelief in us no matter how complete and passionate the faith that imbues us, there is always in the Church on earth a measure of failure and perversion both in its hearing of the Word and in its response to it. The Church is by its nature not only the Church of God, but a Church of men. They are called out of the world to have their life in sole allegiance to God, and yet this Church which they now constitute, in order to be the servant of God's revelation to men, has to remain in the world, intimately involved in man's life in every age. The man who is called into the Church does not cease to be a man of his own time and place, sharing the culture of his time and determined outwardly and inwardly by the world of his time. Deep in his own nature he recognizes the hidden roots of those developments which are written large in the history of his age. Therefore, he finds himself unable to detach himself from the context of the larger community of which he is a part, and, like Isaiah, knows in himself not only sin and unbelief that are his conscious personal responsibility, but also a deeper sin and unbelief that he shares with his community. There are blindnesses in every age of which no one is conscious because they are so widespread that they are recognized as normal. There is unbelief that so completely captures the mind of an age that it goes unchallenged even within the Church. There are sins that establish themselves so securely in a civilization that no one any longer considers them to be sins and they may become knit into the very texture of the Church. All three of these statements could be illustrated profusely from history; in fact, the witness of history is that usually the most dangerous blindnesses, unbelief, and sin in the Church remain unrecognized until they have brought disaster upon it.

There is need, therefore, for yet another service of God in the Church, a discipline in which the Church will mount the watchtower and scan its life and faith in all directions, in order to detect the presence of blindness, unbelief, unfaithfulness, and sin, and give warning before it is too late. This is the task of theology. Theology is simply the Church taking with complete seriousness the question of its own existence and inquiring with the utmost thoroughness at what points it is failing to be the Church of God. And a theology that knows that the question of truth and falsehood within the Church is likely at any moment to be a question of life or death for the Church pursues its task with urgency and refuses to be considered a leisurely and rather impractical academic occupation, somewhere apart from the real life and work of the Church.

The peril of the Church is always from within. If it is the Church of God, rightly hearing God's Word to it in the gospel, and responding to it with an unconditional faith, there is no power in all the earth that can destroy it. It does not need to fear its adversaries, however powerful they may be. But let it become something other than the Church of God in itself and at once it is vulnerable to its enemies. Thus, the peril of the Church today is not to be seen in the political systems of Communism or Fascism, or in the growing strength of a humanism that has no place in it for Christianity, or in the secularism of our age. These are enemies that it is very easy to recognize, and it is not difficult to get Christian people roused against them. But the inevitable consequence is a false confidence. Convinced that the Church's enemies are these hostile forces beyond its walls, members and ministers alike keep their eyes concentrated in the wrong direction and have no eyes to see the inner betrayal that is a far more immediate and ominous danger. The enemy from without has power to destroy the Church only when he finds the Church confused in its faith, vague concerning its own nature and destiny, and no longer clear in its own mind about what it owes to either God or man. The first task of theology is to expose this confusion and uncertainty of the Church concerning itself and to inquire how the Church can most truly be the Church.

The function of theology is therefore necessarily a critical one, and the thoroughness and fearlessness with which it performs its critical task will be the measure of its service to the Church. This critical note has been conspicuously lacking in much American theology. A book or article on a theological subject commonly takes the form of a monologue by one theologian and rarely becomes part of a living dialogue in which theologians of the Church discuss with each other the life and death questions of the Church's existence. Each theologian stands upon his own place of eminence and declares what he considers to be the truth of the matter, but he refrains from entering into debate with those, who may live quite close to him, who say something quite different. A really critical theologian would be likely in this polite atmosphere to be regarded as brutal and intolerant. The theological conversation within the Church must not, at all costs, offend anyone! But the question is whether, on such a basis, theology can perform its rightful function within the Church. A theology that contents itself with positive instruction and leaves aside its critical task is a theology which has ceased to be a watchman over the Church's life and has left the Church defenseless against the perils of its own confusion and unfaithfulness.

The Departments of Theology

The task of theology is so great that it must be broken down into its component parts, but, in this process of separation, no part should be allowed to lose its participation in and relationship to the total task of theology. Whether a man's responsibility lies in Old Testament studies, or in systematic theology, or in homiletics, or in Christian education, he is before all else a critical theologian of the Church, pursuing work that must be constantly kept in close relation to the work of all other departments, and he must constantly be asking what significance his researches have and what contribution they make toward the recovery by the Church of its true nature and destiny.

Since the revelation from which the Church has its life is known only through the Scriptures of the Old and New Testaments, one department of theology must be devoted to the investigation of the Scriptures in order to determine ever afresh on behalf of the Church what the word of God was that first sounded in the ears and hearts of prophets and apostles. It is merely a matter of expediency that the Biblical department divides naturally in two, because of the difficulty of any one man's mastering the linguistic and historical details of both Old and New Testaments. It is a division only of work, and not of subject, for the two departments must have the same indivisible subject, the revelation of God to his Church through the Scriptures.

God's word in Scripture does not consist of two neatly separated words, an Israelite or Jewish one and a Christian one. It is one Word, incarnate in Jesus Christ, and yet at the same time the Word to which the Old Testament bears essential witness, so that Jesus Christ cannot be torn apart from his context in the Israel of God without making him something other than he is, and the Old Testament cannot be separated from the revelation in Jesus Christ without ceasing to be Christian Scripture. Thus, in theology, Old and New Testament departments dare not pursue their subjects in isolation from each other, for neither of the Testaments can be rightly understood apart from the other. Many of the developments in Old Testament scholarship during the past century would have been very different from what they were if the Old Testament scholar had remained aware that he was primarily not an expert in Oriental languages, literature, and history, but a theologian of the Church, investigating on behalf of the Church the nature of the Word of God in the Old Testament portion of the Christian Scriptures. When he became primarily an Orientalist and ceased to regard himself as a theologian, he not only robbed his work of its significance for the Church and theology, but he left vacant an important department in theology, and robbed the whole of theology of a vital and indispensable element in its knowledge of the Biblical revelation. The same can be said of New Testament scholarship, in so far as the same development took place in it. Today in both departments there is a recovery of their basic theological character, and naturally an enhancement of their significance for the Church. But there is still a widespread failure to recognize the essential unity of the two departments. It is impossible for an Old Testament scholarship that confines its attention exclusively to the Old Testament to make clear to the Church how the God whom it knows and serves in Jesus Christ continues to speak to it through the Old Testament Scriptures.

The life of the Church is that through it the same God who made himself known to the prophets and apostles and who was incarnate in Jesus Christ may continue to reveal himself to man today, that he may indwell his Church in all the fullness of his power, truth, and love, and that in his living Word he may come to man ever anew in judgment and in mercy. The revelation of God is, therefore, not only in the Scriptures, but also in the Church. In so far as the Church is in reality the body of Christ and the servant of the Word, God's word is alive in it; not a new or different revelation, for that would make of the Church something other than the body of Christ, but the same revelation and the same living God who is known in the Scriptures. It is not sufficient merely that the Scriptures exist and are available to men. God did not entrust his gospel to a book, but to a fellowship of disciples in whose hearts he writes his word and whom he empowers to be his witnesses by his indwelling Spirit. Alongside the word of God in the Scriptures and wholly dependent upon it, there must be the word of God in the preaching and teaching and action and entire life of the Church, not just an interpretation of the word of the Scriptures — for then we should be like the Church of the scribes, with none of the authority or power of the living Word and Spirit of God — but the same Word and the same Spirit, which means the same God speaking and being heard in modern terms in our modern situation.

This revelation of God in the Church leaves its very human record in preaching, teaching, missionary activity, charitable projects, and all else that makes up the life and activity of the Church. Theology, however, has to ask the question, Is that which is found in the Church the genuine manifestation and fruitage of God's Presence which makes it a true Church, or is it at certain points something else and therefore a falsification of the revelation, resulting in a perversion of the Church from its true nature? To this question the department of systematic theology addresses itself, and, since the Church's message and life comes to clearest expression in the doctrines that are most widely held within it, systematic theology addresses itself to the critical examination of the doctrines in which the Church's life is rooted. To it the Church looks for leadership in an inquiry that concerns the entire Church, a searching investigation of the question of truth and error in the Church's message and principles. To it, also, the Church looks for a comprehensive statement of its doctrine, in which every detail is set in its proper relationship within the whole. But because a fallible human Church, involved as it is in a sinful human world, finds itself always in a dilemma between truth and falsehood, the task of systematic theology must ever be an intensively critical one, and even its most comprehensive statement of doctrine can have in it no finality but must provide the material for the next stage in its critical task.

The historical department in theology is the handmaid of the Biblical and systematic. Neither of them can function without its assistance. Nothing is known of the revealing activity of God either in the Scriptures or in the Church, apart from historical records. The task of investigating those records in order to reconstruct the events of the past and so to enable us to see what actually happened is the task of the historian. Usually the Old and New Testament departments include within their scope the history of their periods, and the department of Church history concerns itself mainly with the post-Biblical periods. Again, it is important to recognize that this is an artificial division and that the history of the Church comprehends both Biblical and post-Biblical periods. It is all of a piece, and the right understanding of any one part of it depends upon seeing it as a whole. It is the story of the human instrument through which God has chosen to reveal himself and to carry forward his redemptive purpose in the life of man. It is a story of faithfulness and unfaithfulness, of a Church that responded in faith to God and of a Church that rebelled in pride against God. Thus, in the history we see those who have gone before us wrestling with the very questions and facing the same dilemmas, or others very like them, that we have to face in our own day. History is the Church's memory of itself, the repository of its past experiences, and therefore, the dimension of depth in its existence, and whatever question the Church and the Christian consider in theology, or whatever decision they have to make in their life, they must bring to bear upon it the total experience of the past.

Theology, however, has not completed its task when it has dealt with the revelation as it is heard in the Scriptures and as it sounds in and through the Church; it has next to turn its attention to the

Church's response to the revelation in worship, preaching, teaching, missions, and in its total obedience to God in common life. Revelation and response belong very intimately together. It is worthy of consideration that the psalms, which by their nature are not primarily the word of God to man but rather the word of man in response to God, are also one form of the word of God. It is the Spirit of God dwelling in the human heart that alone makes it possible for a man to respond rightly to God, and in the prayers of confession and thanksgiving and petition that we find in the book of The Psalms, we recognize, not just man's expression of his own spirit, but the Spirit of God in him, bringing to utterance the deep things of his spirit before God. God's coming to man in revelation calls for a corresponding movement of the total being of man toward God. God comes to man that man may come to him. The Church has its life in the twofold movement, and theology must concern itself not only with the revelation, but also with the response.

The departments of theology that have to do with the Church's response are usually given the title " practical," because every aspect of the response involves the Church in practices of some kind. There can be no response without action. Therefore, practical theology is the study of the Church in action, the critique of its practices in the past, the determination on principle of what should be its practices in the present, and the training of its ministry to be guides into a right fulfillment of its nature in response to God in the future. It is clear, therefore, that " practical " does not mean " untheological." The practical considerations are as thoroughly theological as those that arise in the Biblical, systematic, and historical departments of theology. Every theological concern comes here to its practical expression. But it can be understood only when it is traced to its Biblical and theological roots. All the basic theological questions have to be asked afresh in the practical field, but now there is the additional urgency in them that their implications for the Church's practice are very clearly seen.

This involvement of the practical disciplines in theology needs to be emphasized, for there is a widespread impression that the practical departments need not be so seriously or deeply theological as the others, and they have suffered severely from the lack of theologians in them. Often competence in theology has ranked low among the qualifications of men being considered for appointments to practical departments. Worship, education, homiletics, pastoral care, and missions have been regarded as techniques in which men must be trained, and the call has been for the experienced technician, rather than for the theologian. There has even been a suspicion that too much knowledge of theology will unfit a man for effective work in the practical field. Nothing could better illustrate the unfortunate and debilitating cleft within the Church between thought and action. The cleft is only too plainly to be seen in many theological seminaries and it is not surprising that it should appear at various points in the life of the Church, with serious consequences both for theology and for the existing practices of the Church.

The departments of practical theology correspond to the elements in the Church's response to God. First, therefore, must be named liturgics, which attempts, in the light of what the Church's worship has been in the past and upon the basis of a Biblical definition of the nature of worship, to give guidance in the ordering of the Church's worship in the present. It asks the question, How shall a Christian congregation most truly, most completely, and most fruitfully respond to God in worship? And it brings the whole of theology, Biblical, systematic, historical, and practical, to bear upon this question. Where liturgics degenerates into an uncritical exposition of, and training in, the liturgy of one denomination, it merely reinforces the tendency already so strong in the Church to do no more than maintain the form of worship that at some point in the past was established in this particular part of the Church. Thus, for instance, the Puritan abolition of all liturgy, which left the congregation no active participation in the worship except in the singing of several psalms or hymns, has remained unquestioned in wide areas of Protestantism, even though it represents a development in worship quite contrary to the convictions of Reformers such as Luther, Calvin, and Knox. The Church, for the healthy ordering and development of its worship, requires among the theological disciplines one that will give its attention critically and constructively to this question. Within its scope, of course, is included also the administration of the sacraments.

The second element in the Church's response to God is its offering of itself for the service of God's Word. But this ministry of the Word is of such a magnitude that it requires several departments in theology for its investigation and development. First, the preaching of the Word requires a department of homiletics, which examines the question of how the revelation, which is heard in the Scriptures and received by the Church as the very source of its life, may sound into the life of our time from the lips of the preacher as nothing less than the word of God to man. Homiletics brings the entire apparatus of theology to bear upon this one point — how, through the words of a minister of the Church, there is to be a revelation *now* of the living, redeeming God, who is man's only Lord. A homiletics that busies itself only with the apparatus of preaching, and fails to venture beyond the " how " of the matter, leaves men, however polished their manner and style, incompetent to preach. It also leaves them in vagueness and confusion about the relation of what they have learned in the other departments of theology to the actual work of preaching. The lament of theologians continually is that so much that is common knowledge among the theologians of the Church fails to get out beyond the theological seminary into the Christian congregations. Congregations may be, in some respects, at least fifty years behind the theologians. There is a failure in communication. But what few seem to realize is that the failure stems from the gap between the department of homiletics and the Biblical and systematic departments in the seminaries. The Biblical and systematic theologians so rarely teach with the situation of the preacher before their minds, and the teacher of homiletics so rarely deals with preaching as the final practical expression of the same Word of revelation with which Biblical and systematic theology have been concerned.

Secondly, the teaching of the Word requires a department of Christian education. It must be closely related to the other departments, for the work of education is carried forward in worship, in preaching, and in pastoral relationships. There have been times when preaching has been the most effective force for education in the Church. And certainly in an earlier day in Presbyterianism, the pastoral calls, during which the minister examined the members of the family, old and young, on their knowledge of the faith, had a powerful influence educationally. Education is also an important factor in missions and evangelism. Equally essential is the relation with the Biblical, systematic, and historical departments, for an education that divorces itself from them will be an education that swiftly loses its roots in the historic Christian tradition and is tempted to find its context in some other and seemingly more desirable tradition. In short, it is in danger of becoming something other than *Christian* education. We shall see in the next chapter how, during the past half century, this divorce of Christian education from its true context in the Church and theology actually took place in some quarters and led to developments that, however impressive they might be educationally, were theologically irresponsible. But before churchmen, and particularly theologians, wax too scornful about such developments, they should consider their own responsibility in having neglected to find for Christian education its proper place in the structure of theology. There were theologians fifty years ago who even contested the right of a Christian education that was determined to be seriously educational to remain within the Church. The divorce between Christian education and theology was as much the fault of theologians who were educationally blind as it was of educators who were theologically blind.

The teacher of the Word requires the same grounding Biblically, systematically, and historically, as the preacher of the Word. The teacher and the preacher have a common ministry. They serve the same revelation of God which comes to them from the Scriptures and through the total witness of the Church. Both stand under the same peril of having their ministry destroyed by the substitution of some other revelation for the revelation of God, and, therefore, both need to be trained to be alert and critical theologians. Theological error or confusion in the teaching of the Church is quite as destructive as theological error or confusion in the preaching of the Church. Also, it should be recognized that in the vast majority of congregations the preacher has no educational director alongside him but is required to provide the church with its lead in education. The department of Christian education therefore must bring the entire discipline of theology to bear upon the educational problem, and, in its exploration of what it means for the Church to be an effective educational agency in the service of the Word, it must not only be ready to learn from those who are investigating the fields of educational psychology and technique from a secular point of view but must conduct its own careful researches in the light of its own objects and aims. Even in educational psychology the presuppositions of the investigator have an influence upon both his observations and his conclusions. The Christian educator has thus to be on guard lest, in taking over supposedly scientific conclusions from the secular educator, he take over also, unconsciously, certain unacknowledged, non-Christian, or even anti-Christian assumptions, which the secular educator did not deduce from his observations but brought to them from some other source.

The department of pastoral theology deals with the ministry of the Word as it is exercised, not in a formal preaching or teaching situation, but in that intimate personal contact in which it is focused upon the existence of one person or one family. It is a ministry that may belong not only to the preacher but also to the teacher, and not to them alone, but also to the ordinary church member. It is the most difficult situation in which to have a Christian ministry, because in it one no longer has the protection of a pulpit or of a class to shield him from the stark reality of human need. One is exposed to the doubts, the urgent questions, the distressing tangles, the sins, of another soul, and thereby has his own faith and knowledge put to the severest test. It is well to remember that the pastoral ministry is still the ministry *of the Word*. The relief of doubts, the answering of the questions, the unraveling of the tangles, will all lead nowhere unless the person being ministered to learns that beneath all problems is ever the problem of God, and that no solution can amount to anything unless the living God, who is Father, Son, and Holy Spirit, is found as the answer to the soul's need. The person in need must be led to the point where he begins really to hear God speaking into the deep places of his life through the word of Scripture. In order to understand the person to whom he ministers, the pastor makes use of all that he can learn about the human soul from psychology and sociology, from literature, and from his own experiences of life. But everything he learns he brings under the light where alone he rightly knows either himself or his fellow man, the light of

God's presence in his Word and Spirit, for the revelation of God is always at the same time the revelation of man.

Under the influence of psychiatry there has been a tendency in some quarters of the Church for pastors to think of themselves as semiprofessional Christian psychiatrists and for pastoral theology to concern itself more with psychology than with the Bible or theology. On this road there is danger of a rather dilettante soul-tinkering. The young graduate, with his courses in psychology, and perhaps with some clinical training, is ready to take on the soul problems of modern man! He has not bothered much with his Biblical and theological subjects, and he does not expect to do much in preaching, for he is fascinated with the possibilities of pastoral counseling. In the light of such developments there is need for pastoral theology to be redefined within the context of the Church and in relation to the other theological disciplines. It cannot do its work alone, for the private counseling of individuals best succeeds when those individuals are also receiving a ministry through the worship and preaching of the Church, and through participation in an educational group. The ultimate question is not, Can this individual find a solution to his immediate problem? but rather, Can this individual find the destiny God has for him in Jesus Christ, and can he find his place in the Church of God?

The departments of missions and evangelism focus upon two special responsibilities of the Church in its service of the Word. The history of missions is actually a part of Church history, the entire history of the Church being the history of a mission. It has been cut apart from its larger context usually as a result of a failure of the Church historian to include within the scope of his subject the history of the modern missionary movement. The separation has the unfortunate result of creating the impression that the Church is a mission in its enterprise abroad but not a mission in the older established work at home. The task of a department of missions in a critical theology should be to turn the searchlight of theology upon the vast enterprise of missions, asking the question with earnestness, Is the Church truly the Church in its outreach into these foreign lands with their different civilizations? It would be of great service to the Church and to those training for service in missions if in our seminaries the entire missionary enterprise were examined critically and constructively in the light of what we discover the Church to be in the Scriptures and in history.

A department of evangelism focuses upon the problem of how the Church is to fulfill its mission in a community where the Christian congregation has become walled off from the non-Christian community and has no effective means of breaking through the wall of separation. It is difficult for it to operate as a separate department, for at the root of the problem is the loss of their evangelical character by the preaching and teaching of the Church. A nonevangelizing Church is the product of a moralistic preaching and teaching which leaves Christians with the idea that they have fulfilled their responsibility when they have lived good lives and been faithful in attending and contributing to the Church. Therefore the main training in evangelism must be done in the departments of homiletics and Christian education. The demand for a separate department may well be the consequence of a failure in these two departments to establish the evangelical nature of all preaching and teaching. Perhaps it would justify its separate existence by pointing to the acute problem of training men and women members of the Church for an active Christian ministry, but surely that must be the goal of the whole program of education in the Church. It is hard to grant to a department of evangelism more than a temporary existence in the disciplines of theology as a protest against the neglect of their true nature and function by other departments, and as a means of fastening the attention of the Church upon one of its most urgent problems. In a healthy theology there would be no need for a department of evangelism, for all the departments would be conscious of their responsibility before God for the recovery by the Church of its nature and power as an instrument in the hand of God for the conversion of the world.

Where the department of Christian ethics belongs in the structure of theology is a difficult question to answer. It faces the final decisive issue on which everything hinges, the response of the Church in obedience to God in the totality of life. Let this response be lacking and the Church is one gigantic hypocrisy. The questions God will use to search our hearts before his judgment seat will not have to do primarily with our worship or doctrine but with our actions in relation to our fellow men, in which alone the character of our worship and doctrine are evident. Because Christian ethics has to do with this question of action, it might well be considered a department in practical theology. Ethics is in the most definite way Christian theology directed specifically to the problem of what the Church and Christians do in all the spheres of their life. But because belief and action are so closely related, the action being determined by the underlying doctrine and the doctrine being clearly evident only in the action, Christian ethics must always be kept in indissoluble unity with systematic theology and may even be considered a department within systematic theology. This is simply one further and final instance of the unity of all the departments of theology and of the harm that is done to them when they are allowed to go apart from each other into a false independence. Each has its health only within the total family.

The purpose of this chapter has been to draw out the full picture of the theological family, that the place of Christian education within it may be seen with clearness, and that the involvement of Christian education in the total structure of theology may come to recognition. It has far-reaching implications, not only for Christian education, but for all the other disciplines.

3

HOW CAME WE HERE?

S O confused is the educational situation in the Church that we may easily be guilty of harsh and uncharitable judgments unless we understand something of the interplay of forces and ideas during the past two centuries. How does it come to pass that one deeply earnest man, after a lifetime serving the Church in education, finds himself proposing a radical break with the historic Christian tradition, while at the opposite extreme an equally earnest man refuses to let anything be taught in his church school except Bible lessons, excluding even a series on the history of the Church? There are conflicting traditions in the church school, sometimes interwoven in a single situation, and all of us have been influenced by them from the time we first attended church school. Therefore, if we are to understand not only the situation as it exists in the Church, but, more specifically, our own inclinations and preferences, we need to trace the developments of the past.

BACKGROUND IN BIBLE AND CHURCH

Little is known concerning the provision for education in the Biblical period, perhaps because it had its locus so largely in the home. In Israel the parents were charged with the responsibility of educating their family in the true faith, and there were religious festivals in the home which gave opportunity regularly for calling attention to essentials of that faith. In the time of Jesus there were synagogue schools, elementary and advanced, in which boys first learned to read and memorize the Scriptures and then went on to problems of interpretation. In the Early Christian Church, new em-

46

phasis was placed upon teaching because of the necessity that converts should be thoroughly instructed in their faith. The tradition of
teaching in the home continued. So also in Christian preaching the
synagogue tradition of a teaching ministry continued. But the catechetical classes represented an entirely new development, and, during the first three centuries, played a large part in training Christians
in the essentials of their faith. They became, in time, the theological
schools of the Church. But after the fourth century they faded out of
existence.

The medieval period represents an all-time low for education in
the Church, and the general neglect was reflected in the ignorance of
many of the clergy. The emphasis upon the sacraments as the essential means of grace led to a decline and even to an abandonment of
preaching, so that the people, uninstructed in the Scriptures in worship, became incapable of teaching their own children in the home.
Schools attached to monasteries reached a few youths, but rarely any
except those destined for a special vocation in the Church.

The Reformation Churches, therefore, with their restoration of
the preaching of the Word of God to the center of worship, with
their reinstitution of catechetical instruction before confirmation,
and with their insistence upon the duty of every parent to instruct
the members of his family in the Bible and doctrine, were actually
returning to the order that existed in the churches of the first three
centuries. But, like all such returns, it picked up the lines of development and carried them farther than they had been carried before.
A Church reformed according to the Word of God in Scripture depended for its health upon the ability of its members to read and
understand the Scriptures for themselves. The Bible, therefore, was
translated into the language of the common man by Tyndale,
Luther, and others. But that was not sufficient unless the common
man was trained to read. So the Reformers were propelled into new
developments in education. In Geneva, Calvin founded schools to
provide an elementary education for all, and in that education the
religious and the cultural elements were united. John Knox, under
Calvin's influence, initiated similar educational reforms in Scotland.
His aim, which was not always realized, was a school in every parish,
and a schoolmaster alongside the parish minister, in close co-opera-

tion with him. The provision thus made in church, home, and school for education in the Christian faith was much more comprehensive than anything to be found in our modern situation. The character of the education provided may at many points have left much to be desired, but no man can speak disrespectfully of the Reformers in their concern for education.

Some of these sixteeth century institutions, particularly in Europe, have persisted into the modern situation. The school in which religious instruction is combined with general education is found both in Britain and on the Continent. It was the order also in colonial America, and gave way only gradually to the present order in which religious and general education are almost completely separated. Catechetical instruction on a major scale, with regular classes over a period of two years, and with a minister as teacher, still retains its place in many European churches. In Presbyterian churches the custom continued until the middle of the nineteenth century, and in some quarters still continues, of the minister on his pastoral calls examining the members of the family on their knowledge of the Bible and the catechism, a practice that served to keep parents active, at least in some degree, at their educational task.

The modern period opens near the end of the eighteenth century. By that time the developments that began with the Reformation had spent their force, and for some generations had lost their influence in the population at large. The original surge of new life and thought in the Church had hardened into the more scholastic and static forms of Puritanism, or had been dissolved by the acids of eighteenth century Rationalism. The wars of religion that devastated so much of Europe left many people with a decided distaste for religious enthusiasm, and made them relish the advantages and particularly the comfortableness of a religion that claimed to be little more than sanctified common sense. Then, as the eighteenth century advanced, there came the evangelical revival, spreading rapidly through Britain and America, with corresponding movements on the continent of Europe. At first its strength was in mass meetings, to which came thousands who had never had a chance to hear with clearness the word of the gospel. But, as the thousands of converts were formed into churches or swarmed into existing congregations, the situation was ripe for a work of education which would follow upon the work of the evangelist. It was in this situation that the Sunday School movement was born.

THE SUNDAY SCHOOL MOVEMENT

In 1780, in Gloucester, England, Robert Raikes began his first "Ragged School," that he might do for the illiterate children of Gloucester what John Knox in his day did for the illiterate children of Scotland. But these children of Gloucester had to have their schooling on Sunday. The program consisted mainly of reading, writing, and arithmetic, but there were also Bible lessons, and the aim of the entire training was to fit these children for an intelligent Christian life. In England at that time, and far on into the nineteenth century, there was no adequate provision for the education of the children from low-income homes. Therefore, the movement begun by Raikes spread rapidly from city to city and gave to thousands of children a chance in life they would never otherwise have had. In Scotland, where there was already provision for elementary education for all classes, the movement took a different direction, being confined to religious instruction, and in this form it was soon to be found both on the Continent and in America.

Two things happened at the very beginning of this development to fasten upon it characteristics that it has retained in some degree ever since. Many in high places of influence in the Church and society in England regarded the Sunday Schools as signs of a stirring among the common people that might have revolutionary implications. What would happen when these ragged children of the proletariat became educated? They would no longer be willing to keep their humble place in society. One had only to look across the channel to France where the blood of the best people was running red in the streets, all because of a dangerous teaching that led the common man to think that he was worth as much as any aristocrat. The clergy were scandalized that men and women who had little more than their evangelical zeal were presuming to set themselves up as Christian teachers in the Sunday Schools, and that they operated completely outside the scope and authority of the Church. A religious development uncontrolled by the clergy might lead to some very undesirable results. As a consequence of such fears and opposition, Sunday School workers were subject to persecution in some communities and the movement in turn took on a certain anti-clerical character.

There was, however, one quarter in which the Sunday School received an enthusiastic welcome and that was from the churches that had come into existence as a fruit of the evangelical revival or had been strongly influenced by it. The clergy and the aristocrats who looked with disfavor on the Sunday School were also opposed to the followers of Wesley and Whitefield. Nothing can do more to throw people into alliance than to have a common enemy. Moreover, the evangelical churches, with their thousands of converts, required an educational development to carry forward the work that had been begun. So the two came together, and as a consequence of this alliance the Sunday School became strongly anchored in the tradition of the evangelical revival. The influence is to be traced in the conception of its purpose as an instrument for evangelizing the young, the character of the hymns associated with it which did so much to fix its tone, and also the theology which was long to be dominant in it, often in sharp antithesis to the theology of the Church in which the particular Sunday School had its home.

Very early the Sunday School lost its character as a school for the illiterate children of non-Christian parents and became a school for children both of Church families and of families outside the Church. When it began in America, shortly after its origin in England, it took this form. The moment was propitious for its spread in the new United States of America. In colonial America, religious instruction had been combined with general education in the schools of the land, but through various influences public education in the new nation was soon to be secularized and a sharp line of separation drawn between Church and State. The churches could no longer look to the school to instruct children in the Christian faith, and, as the secularization of the schools advanced between 1787 and 1847, Christians found in the Sunday School a ready-made instrument to carry forward this necessary work. Also, the evangelical revival, which was as powerful in America as in England, was not slow to seize upon this valuable new institution. As early as 1790, Sunday

Schools were sanctioned by the Methodist Conference of South Carolina. There was clerical opposition in America, parallel to that experienced in England, serving to create in many minds an antithesis between the Sunday School and the Church, and to fix upon the movement, in some measure, an anticlericalism. Thus, the American Sunday School Union, founded in 1824, would permit no clergyman to be a member of its board, and, within the Churches, the tradition was formed that in the Sunday School the leadership should rest entirely with laymen and not with ministers. Under the auspices of the American Sunday School Union missioners went through the Western states as they opened up and established Sunday Schools, which were often the only Christian agencies in the communities. These schools later grew into churches. Their purpose was more purely evangelistic than educational at first, but they were equipped to follow their evangelism with an educational program.

The form of the Sunday School session became fixed at an early stage and the tradition has persisted in various countries essentially unchanged to the present day. It is curious to read in Hauck's *Realencyklopädie für Protestantische Theologie und Kirche,* published in 1903, a description of what was being done in German Sunday Schools shortly after the movement spread to Germany. It took root first in the city of Hamburg, in 1825, but had its most rapid expansion after 1863, when Woodruff, an American Sunday School leader, visited Germany. By 1899 there were 400,000 children in 1,700 schools in Germany. In a typical session there was first an opening period of worship, with emphasis upon singing. The children then divided into classes for a twenty- to twenty-five-minute lesson period. This was followed by a closing period, in which the superintendent added some remarks, papers were distributed, and library books were given out. Church leaders were finding it a problem that in the Sunday Schools the inclination was to use a cheaper type of hymn than was customary in the Church, so that the Sunday School and the Church had differing traditions in hymnody.

This might well be a description of many American and Canadian Sunday Schools in the mid-twentieth century. It helps us to realize how early an independent Sunday School tradition developed and how static it has been. Generation after generation of leaders have felt duty bound to carry on the tradition as it was originally established, and some have regarded any deviation from it as the death of the Sunday School. This has been a major factor in preventing progress in educational work in many sections of the Church.

Horace Bushnell

While the Sunday School movement was still in its early stages in America, a book appeared that tried to turn educational interest in another direction. In 1847, Horace Bushnell published the first draft of his *Christian Nurture,* which was to be rewritten and republished a number of times in succeeding years. Bushnell was in reaction against a type of narrowly evangelistic Christianity which was widespread in New England and closely associated with many of the Sunday Schools. According to the doctrine of these earnest people, every child, regardless of the context in which he was nurtured, continued as a creature of sin until the time of a sudden conversion. Therefore, the one thing to be done with the child was to bring every means to bear to effect a conversion, and, until such conversion took place, the child was to be regarded and treated as not yet a Christian. Some even questioned whether it was of any use to try to educate children before conversion. After all, how could they understand anything of the things of God until they knew God by faith? The work of the Sunday School was thus primarily to convert children. Bushnell protested that this not only did violence to the realities in the life of the child, but was contrary to the clear teaching of the Bible itself. The child is not to be torn apart from the context of the home and treated as a completely independent individual. The home is an organism in which child and parent are part of each other so that they share a common life, and if there is Christian faith in the parent, the child will begin to participate in it from the time of his birth. " A pure, separate, individual man, living *wholly* within, and from himself, is a mere fiction. No such person ever existed or ever can " (*Christian Nurture,* page 31). Thus, the child who has grown up into the faith of a Christian home cannot be treated as though he were an unbeliever.

Bushnell, in support of his thesis, pointed to the baptism of households in the New Testament, particularly those of Stephanas and the Philippian jailer, and to Paul's teaching that, in a family, a believing wife sanctifies an unbelieving husband. To him, the family is God's loving provision that the child from birth may be a child of faith, bringing God's mercy and goodness and truth into the child's life long before he is able to make choices for himself. " It would certainly be very singular if Christ Jesus in a scheme of mercy for the world had found no place for infants and little children; more singular still, if he had given them the place of adults; and worse than singular, if he had appointed them to years of sin as the necessary preparation for his mercy " (page 54).

So anxious was Bushnell to establish the fact of the unity of the family in belief and unbelief, that he pushed his argument too far, and tended to portray the relationship of parent to child as though it were so direct as to be impersonal. " Their character is yet to be born, and in you is to have its parentage. Your spirit is to pass into them, by a law of transition that is natural, and well-nigh irresistible " (page 64). " The family is such a body that a power over character is exerted therein *which cannot properly be called influence.* We commonly use the term ' influence ' to denote a persuasive power, or a governmental power, exerted purposely and with a conscious design to effect some result in the subject. In maintaining the organic unity of the family, I mean to assert that a power is exerted by parents over children, not only when they teach, encourage, persuade, and govern, but without any purposed control whatever. The bond is so intimate that they do it unconsciously, and undesignedly — they must do it. Their character, feelings, spirit, and principles must propagate themselves, whether they will or not " (page 92). " Your character is a stream, a river, flowing down upon your children, hour by hour " (page 118).

We can go all the way with Bushnell in recognizing the validity of what he is describing, the continuous unconscious influence of the parents' character and convictions in shaping the life of the child, and yet draw back from his conclusion, that the child's life is so directly determined by the life of the parent that the parent's faith inevitably becomes the faith of the child. Even when the relationship is unconscious, it is personal, with action and response, and the unconscious response of the child may be to react against what meets him in the parent, rather than to be passively determined by it. Also, it is dangerous to suggest that one can become a Christian merely by growing up in a Christian home. Only too often the off-spring of Christian parents move on into adult life with only the faith they have received at second hand from their parents and without having come to a firsthand knowledge of what it means to believe personally in God as their Father Almighty, in Jesus Christ as their Saviour, and in the Holy Spirit as God coming now to in-dwell their entire being through faith. What the child receives from Christian parents is neither to be denied its validity nor is it to be made a substitute for the personal faith of the Christian disciple. But certainly Bushnell is right in insisting that a conversionism that refuses to consider anyone a Christian until he has had a cer-tain type of "conversion experience" is making of faith something other than it is in the New Testament. There the decisive thing is not the having of experiences, but the willingness to have Jesus Christ as absolute Lord over one's life.

THE BIRTH OF THE RELIGIOUS EDUCATION MOVEMENT

Bushnell's teaching found acceptance in some quarters, but the main stream of the Sunday School movement was already com-mitted in another direction by the closeness of its tie with the re-vivalistic movement. It moved on its way, spreading through all the churches and retaining tenaciously the characteristics that it had assumed in its beginnings. It was usually more concerned with con-version than with education. Most schools were completely un-graded, and often the greater part of the hour was spent in an audi-torium with all ages of children together with young people and adults. In 1872, the Uniform Lesson system was adopted, which greatly facilitated the preparation of lesson materials, but fastened upon the Sunday School a system in which, on any given Sunday, the same passage of Scripture was to be taught to four-year-old children as was to be taught to adults. The approach to Scripture was usually literalistic, for by the latter half of the nineteenth cen-tury the evangelical movement had hardened into fundamentalism;

and those who were dominant in the Sunday School movement had become hostile to the whole of the historical and critical movement in Biblical interpretation.

It is not surprising that, as the nineteenth century drew to a close, there was an increasing dissatisfaction in the churches with the character of the Sunday School. In United States, Britain, and the continent of Europe, the theology of most churches was no longer that of the evangelical revival, even where the churches had retained their evangelical concern. The tide of liberalism had swept over Protestantism, leaving nothing the same as it was before. In Europe, Schleiermacher, Ritschl, and Hegel, while diverse in their teachings, were at one in their rejection of orthodoxy and their determination to provide the Church with a substitute doctrine. Coleridge, and a succession of men who drew their inspiration from him, had, in England, helped Christians to put behind them both the barrenness of eighteenth century rationalism and the absurdities of a literalistic and harshly puritanical orthodoxy, and had encouraged them in a reinterpretation of the Christian faith. Some who followed his urging were so anxious to arrive at a faith that would be intellectually acceptable in the nineteenth century world that they retained only a tenuous connection with the Christian gospel, but others, such as Frederick Denison Maurice, held to a warmly evangelical Trinitarian faith, while opening their minds courageously and honestly to the whole range of intellectual problems that now confronted them as Christians. In America, Emerson and the New England liberals, who were in most instances Unitarians, exerted a powerful influence throughout the Church. An optimistic belief in the goodness of man and the perfectibility of human society found ready acceptance on every hand and made men impatient with a theology that told little children they were sinners headed straight for hell unless they were converted. Every advance in education seemed to make the existing order of the Sunday School more intolerable. The membership in the churches became ever more sharply divided between liberals and conversionists, who were eventually to call each other modernists and fundamentalists. In between the extremes were many people who, while they disagreed with the theology of the liberals, were equally repulsed by certain characteristics of the fundamentalists. But they lacked a spokesman or a theologian to give expression to their concern.

Also increasing in the churches was the number of persons for whom the researches of Old and New Testament historical and critical scholars had opened the Scriptures in a new and living way. A literalistic approach was to them a denial of the human historical character of the Bible, and therefore an impediment to the understanding of it. They were no longer satisfied to have children indoctrinated in a literalistic tradition in the Sunday School. They were faced with the decision whether to remove their children from a Sunday School which was giving them an untenable approach to the Bible or to change the character of the Sunday School.

Advances in educational method in the public schools also served to make people critical of the Sunday School. Educators recognized that a system of education that would take into account both the needs of the child and the way in which the child most naturally grows would have to be carefully graded. The different age groups would have to be separated from each other and the curriculum of each group worked out in the light of what, by experience, teachers found the children could most readily and profitably learn. But in the Sunday School, children of widely different ages were lumped together for large portions of the time available, and little attention was given to their differing stages of development. In fact, many of those who worked most enthusiastically in the Sunday School were unconcerned about principles of education and ignored even the simplest laws of learning.

All these forces of protest finally came to expression in America in a great convention, held in Chicago in 1903, for the organization of the Religious Education Association, and the establishment of a new tradition in the Sunday School. One of the moving spirits in this convention was Dr. William Rainey Harper, who was eager to secure the introduction of more intelligent methods of Bible study into the schools of the Church. In its early years, one of the primary aims of the Association was to stimulate a more scholarly use of the Bible. Those who gathered at Chicago, however, were united more by their consciousness of the inadequacy of the Sunday School and their desire for a new day in religious education than by their adherence to any one theological point of view. How divergent the conceptions of religion could be is shown by the fact that one speaker at the convention was John Dewey, who certainly had a different understanding of the word " religion " from that of those who were so anxious for a revived influence of the Bible in the Church. Theologically, the Religious Education Association, both at this time and later, was content to be nebulous. It committed itself to no theology, since it desired to unite all those who were working for a more intelligent approach to problems of religious education, both in the Church and beyond the Church. Never did a movement face a clearer need or begin with greater enthusiasm, but, because it shared, with the earlier Sunday School movement, a loose and indecisive relationship with the Church, and because it assumed falsely that the theological question could be ignored, it was never to fulfill the promise of its beginnings or to do for the Church educationally what needed so badly to be done.

The new movement, originating in an explicit protest against the older tradition in the Sunday School, found itself at once under attack and branded as unchristian. The evangelicals saw in it a threat to the very existence of the Sunday School, and an enemy of the gospel itself. Thus, whoever undertook to introduce a graded program of education in the Church or made use of the results of critical scholarship in his teaching was likely to find himself scourged as a " modernist " and treated as though he were a traitor to the Christian faith. Under such circumstances it was little wonder that the religious education movement became identified with liberal theology, just as a century earlier the Sunday School was drawn into close alliance with the evangelical revival. Under sharp attack from the fundamentalists, the religious educators, wherever their theological allegiance may formerly have lain, found that the only quarter where a warm welcome and enthusiastic support was accorded them was among the liberals. So arose another of those false antitheses which confuse the issues of life for Christians and shatter the unity of the Church. On the one side was a passionate though narrow and literalistic evangelicalism, insisting upon the centrality of the Bible for faith, the converting power of the gospel, and the importance of doctrine, but resisting every effort to secure a more intelligent approach to the interpretation of the Bible and problems of education. On the other side was an equally determined liberalism, insisting that faith must be intellectually honest, that the best literary and historical methods must be used in the investigation of the Bible, and that the Church dare not remain guilty of what elsewhere was recognized as bad educational methods, but less and less interested in a Christianity that takes either the Bible or the Reformation as marking out the direction in doctrine and life in which the Church must go. It was significant that the new movement preferred the name " religious " to that of " Christian."

Each of the two parties could find in the other an abundance of points to attack. The educator reveled in exposing the intellectual absurdity of his opponents' positions. The fundamentalist accused the educators of having abandoned the historic Christian faith. Only too often both were right in their criticisms of each other, but the antithesis had so hardened, and the parties were so completely divided, that they were incapable of profiting by mutual criticism. The validity of their criticisms only served to confirm both in their confidence in the essential rightness of their positions.

There is a danger today, when liberal theology has been so widely repudiated in the Church, that we may lack appreciation of the achievements of men who a half century ago gave valuable service to the cause of education. The theological student opens the books of George A. Coe, the foremost spokesman of religious education, and when he finds a rather thin doctrine of divine immanence, a belief in the naturalness of Christian growth, a blissful confidence in the goodness of man, and a Unitarian conception of Jesus Christ, he is likely to toss the book aside, on the assumption that a structure reared on such untenable theological foundations is unworthy of consideration. He will do well, however, to take up the book again and find what it has to say to him about the educational process. Coe and his colleagues were deeply devoted to the cause of education and pressed their inquiries on behalf of the pupil who is the subject of the Church's education, with a zeal and thoroughness that was new in the history of the Church. At many points their observations were distorted by their theological bias, and their conclusions were reached not, as they thought, by scientific deduction from the facts, but by the interpretation of the facts in the light of the theological viewpoint with which they approached them. Nevertheless, they succeeded in focusing attention upon the pupil and bringing to light a wealth of knowledge for which the Church must be ever in their debt. We shall be more charitable in our attitude toward their theological delinquencies if we recollect that, in the American Church of 1903, the only clear-cut theologies in which men believed with passion were the two extremes of liberalism and fundamentalism. Those who stood somewhere between had, as yet, no spokesman who could make his voice heard on behalf of a valid third possibility.

There is little need to dwell upon the inadequacies of the religious education movement. Shelton Smith, in his *Faith and Nurture* (1941), has laid bare ruthlessly the theological assumptions that were practically universal in the movement. Using as his criterion the essential doctrines of the Christian faith, for which the Church has been recovering an understanding more recently in almost every phase of its theological activity, he demonstrated point by point the incompatibility of the theological tenets of the religious education movement with anything that has ever been recognized by the Church in the past as normative Christianity. The fairness of Smith's conclusions is demonstrated when, in their most recent publications, leaders of the movement, such as Harrison Elliott and Ernest Chave, set their work in the context, not of the Christian Church, but of religion as a universal human phenomenon. When these men call for a complete break with historic Christianity, not at some secondary point but at the center, and wish to discard the essential doctrines which for nineteen centuries have been acknowledged by all sections of the Church, Protestant, Roman Catholic, and Greek Orthodox, as indispensable for a Church that calls itself Christian, they must be prepared to accept the consequences of their decision.

How complete the proposed break is to be is made clear by Chave in his book, *A Functional Approach to Religious Education,* published in 1947. " Two great handicaps to the effective functioning of religion in the modern world," he states, are " sectarianism and supernaturalism " (page v). He later defines these terms in a surprising manner: "Sectarianism" consists in giving exclusive loyalty to one religion, such as Christianity, instead of seeking truth in all religions. Christianity is merely one "sect" among the religions of the world and the day will come when it can be left behind, in order to move upward to a religion that expresses a more comprehensive truth. "Supernaturalism" in Chave's terminology, denotes faith in a personal God, and such belief is classed as outmoded superstition. The only divinity man will ever find is the divinity that is in himself and his world, and that comes to expression in the laws of personal and social development. The Bible, since it is full of supernaturalism, is no longer a readily useful instrument for religious education. It is likely to mislead the growing mind seriously. Instead, we must look to the psychologist, sociologist, and historian, with their scientific investigation of human life, to tell us the truth about man that we need to know. "Religious education cannot look backward for its message, methods, or incentives, but must find them in the growing present" (page 2). It would have been still clearer if he had said specifically what he plainly means — that religious education cannot look backward to the prophets and apostles or to Jesus Christ for its message. Its task is to "co-ordinate the latent spiritual forces of society, giving intelligent leadership and working in close co-operation with social, economic, and political movements, on a world-wide scale" (page vi). "The developing wisdom and idealism of humanity is equal to its problems" (page 3).

The break is complete! Whatever this religion may be, it scorns to be called Christianity, and proponents of it can therefore take no offense if we insist that it is something other than Christianity. Where it lives, the Christian faith ceases to live. It is so completely unrelated to Christianity that it is doubtful if it should even be called a heresy. There could be no clearer indication of the theological confusion that has pervaded wide sections of the Church than the fact that for years teaching of this nature found a considerable response *within the Church*. It involves, not a false teaching about Jesus Christ, but rather a total removal of Jesus Christ from the center of the scene, putting, in place of faith in him, an unlimited faith in the power of human reason to solve all problems.

Chave may represent an extreme development, but that is only because he possesses the type of mind that follows through the implications of a position to its logical conclusions. Starting from the theological assumptions of the religious education movement of a half century ago, we can trace a direct and even an inevitable progress to these conclusions. There have been others in the field who have stopped short of this destination. They have retained their locus within the Christian faith and have tried to combine their Christian insights with the findings of the religious educators. But how indecisively this has been carried through appears when we consider that, until Shelton Smith spoke out in 1941, no volume had appeared in which an educator of the first rank raised a protest against the direction in which the religious education movement was going. Moreover, to this day, there is a conspicuous absence among the writings of the religious educators of any thoroughgoing critique of the movement. The criticism has usually come from men whose vocation in the Church is mainly outside the field of religious education. The religious educators themselves — even those who, in their writings, show the definiteness of their Christian concern — seem disinclined to set their collective house in order theologically.

The contributions of the religious education movement to the ongoing educational programs of the Churches have been very great. The introduction of a graded program was in itself a major achievement and was not carried through without a strenuous struggle. Also, the credit for applying the results of historical-critical Biblical scholarship in church school lessons goes to the religious educators, and where their influence has been weakest the use of the Bible has been the most uncritical and literalistic. They also have been noted for the breadth of their social concern and have forced the Churches to take serious account of the social implications of the gospel. They may not have had the right answers theologically, but they were asking many of the right questions, and a Church that fails to take seriously the questions that they asked will have gone backward.

Unfinished History

Thus far, the modern history of Christian education has fallen neatly into two periods, the second superimposed upon the first, so that both have continued to the present day. The evangelistic period, from 1780 to 1903, does not cease there, but continues parallel with the religious education period from 1903 to the present.

From 1922 until the present, the International Council of Christian Education (since 1952, the Division of Christian Education of the National Council of Churches) has served as a forum of discussion and an agency of co-operation for churches in both traditions. The two streams have mingled in the educational work of most churches, but in varying proportions, so that one church is more in the evangelistic tradition while another is more in that of the religious educators. A consequence of this mingling of traditions has sometimes been a theological confusion, the discordance of the basic ideas behind the two not being recognized. Thus, one might come upon such a phenomenon as an educator with a literalistic view of Scripture which he had drawn from the one tradition, but with a modified form of liberal theology drawn largely from the other. In spite of this mutual influence in the Church at large, the two have remained sharply separated traditions and no other factor has been more divisive in Protestant Churches in America in the last half century.

Now, however, a third period of development has begun that has in it at least the possibility of overcoming the antithesis which divided the earlier two movements. It is all the more hopeful because it has not arisen as an attempt at mediation, trying merely to find a middle point of compromise where two extremes may meet, but as a fresh approach to the total problem of Christian education. This new period may well be named the period of theological recovery. There has been no event of decisive importance to mark its beginning. So slight are the signs of its presence that some leaders in the field speak of it merely as a new " theological emphasis," which has come to season the religious education movement. They are not yet aware of the magnitude of the factors that are involved. The revolution that is at hand is as drastic as that of 1903, and is not likely to be effected without opposition from forces already entrenched.

Harrison Elliott, in his *Can Religious Education Be Christian?*, published in 1941, sprang early to the defense of the religious education movement against what he took to be a theological attack upon the very basis of its existence. But he underestimated his adversary in thinking the attacker to be merely a new and curious theology called "neo-orthodoxy." He should have looked far and wide through the Church and through the various departments of theology — yes, and through the world at large — and have recognized that we have entered a new theological age. We have come into a day in which theological questions are inescapable, and to try to keep religious education untheological is like trying to keep a house at sixty degrees temperature inside while the air pressing into it, every time a door or window is opened, is at one hundred and ten degrees. The pressure for the recovery of theological concern in Christian education has not come in the main from educational leaders. Often their sympathy has pointed directly in the opposite direction. Rather, it has come from underneath, from young people and adults who, in the world of today, are confronted with non-Christian faiths, and demand of their leaders that they tell them plainly what the Christian faith is in distinction to all other faiths. A religious education that refuses to take the essential doctrines of the Christian faith in earnest no longer speaks to the Christian or to man in general, at the point of sharpest urgency.

The decline of liberal theology, upon which religious education had depended for its basic orientation for a half century, was primarily caused by its failure any longer to give a satisfactory explanation to Christians of the realities that confronted them in daily experience. Liberal optimism about human nature was shattered by the outbreak of startling forms of inhumanity within Western civilization. Modern man, confronted by evil in its naked reality, began to find the Biblical description of it once more believable. The idea of an inevitable progress of the human race no longer carried conviction, and the corollary belief, that divinity is to be identified with the natural process by which man moves toward the fulfillment of his destiny, seemed hard to distinguish from a humanism in which all belief in God is abandoned. The bankruptcy of unreconstructed liberalism was impossible to conceal, and the exposure was helped forward by theologians such as Barth and Brunner in Europe, and Reinhold Niebuhr in America.

No single theology has arisen in America to dominate the field left empty by the demolition of liberalism. A variety of theologies have been loosely branded "neo-orthodoxy," which have in common little more than a concern to take seriously the Church's problem of theology. Augustinian, Thomist, Lutheran, Calvinist, disciples of Barth, disciples of Brunner, disciples of the Scandinavian theologians, all are at times lumped together by the defensive liberals, perhaps because all are agreed in their rejection of liberalism. Yet even this rejection is only partial, the new theologians embodying in their thinking such elements of liberalism as its social concern and its sympathy with historical-critical scholarship. It can be stated, however, that little unity exists among the theologies that have developed in reaction to liberalism. Not yet has there been that kind of full-scale discussion of the central doctrines of the Christian faith out of which might come a larger measure of unity, or at least a clarification of the issues. One thing, however, is clear: we are in the midst of a theological revolution in every department of theology, and in every aspect of the Church's life. This is no passing mood of nostalgia for old theologies that will soon fade and leave the way clear for a revival of liberalism. The future will see, not a weakening, but a strengthening and deepening of theological concern.

In 1944 the International Council of Christian Education took cognizance of the changing situation and authorized a Study Committee to consider, among other matters, "the need of a considered statement as to the place of theological and other concepts in Christian education." In the immediately previous years, the Council had been disturbed by stormy debates between traditional religious educators and advocates of a new theological approach. In retrospect, it seems almost unbelievably naïve that anyone should have thought the whole controversy could be resolved by having a committee, representative of all interests, discuss the matter for several years, and draw up "a considered statement." Old Testament science has faced an exactly similar situation: an established approach, which claimed that, to be scientific, it had to be completely untheological, has been challenged by a new approach, which insists that the Old Testament is theological literature and that only an Old Testament science that is theologically responsible is capable of getting at the real content of the Old Testament. The revolution in viewpoint has been proceeding for twenty years now and is forwarded as scholarly works appear that show concretely in the handling of specific problems what is involved in the new approach. How ridiculous it would have been if, ten years ago, a committee had been appointed to issue a statement, after due deliberation, that would settle the question of the place of theological and other concepts in Old Testament science! This is a task, not for a committee of all the talents, holding four meetings of three days each over a period of two years, but for full-scale debate in published researches in the most scholarly fashion possible over a period of twenty to thirty years. And surely Christian educators would be prepared to defend the thesis that a theological revolution in the field of Christian education is a concern of as much magnitude in the Church as a theological revolution in the field of Old Testament science.

The Study Committee reported to the I.C.R.E. in 1946 and 1947, and in the latter year, Paul Vieth, at the request of both bodies, published a popular account of the committee's findings entitled: *The Church and Christian Education*. This book gives evidence of interesting and valuable new developments in Christian education: a recognition of the importance of theological foundations in education, a new emphasis upon the Church as the context within which education takes place, a reaffirmation of the importance of the family, and a concern about the evangelization of the community. Moreover, the theology that Dr. Vieth describes as essential to Christian education, vague as it is at some points, is far removed from the optimistic liberalism of Coe or Chave. Nevertheless, one must say frankly that it is not a book that is likely to spark a theological revolution in the field of Christian education. Dr. Vieth himself cannot be held responsible for this, since he is merely reporting the deliberations and conclusions of the committee. But it must be recognized that from the very first page the report tends to slur over both the issues that have created such sharp conflicts in this field in the past and the questions on which men are divided today. One gets the impression that everything always has been, and still is, remarkably peaceful in this area of the Church's life. No problems confront us that cannot be quite easily settled. At no point is it even admitted that prominent religious educators within the past ten years have advocated theologies that are completely outside the

Christian tradition, or that there are any serious differences between the theologies that underlie the educational programs of the various churches.

It is no accident that, since the publication of this book, the field of Christian education has been remarkably quiet. It would almost appear as though the religious education movement had been able to absorb the " new theological emphasis " into itself and by " taking account of it " to prevent the occurrence of a theological revolution of a nature similar to what has taken place in recent years in the fields of Old Testament, New Testament, systematic theology, and Church history. The new day is to come without repentance or rebirth! No one need ever admit that he was wrong. This is a dangerously false situation, and bodes ill for the future. We get nowhere in any department of theology by slurring issues and crying, " Peace, peace! " where there is no peace. By that road we arrive only at deeper confusion. There can be no escape from the task of rethinking every aspect of the work of Christian education. We need not conceal differences which are actual. A unity that exists only by such concealment is a superficial and unreal thing, which leaves us still tortured by our dividedness beneath the surface. Surely there is a bond of unity in our faith in one Father, one Saviour, and one Spirit, that will give us strength and courage to acknowledge where we are divided from each other in doctrine and practice, and will give us confidence that, if we are honest with God and with each other, and content to work patiently, he will lead us into a much greater unity than we have yet known.

Randolph Crump Miller's *The Clue to Christian Education,* which appeared in 1950, is in direct line with the International Council report. He recognizes that theology has come to stay in Christian education, but does not seem to grasp the magnitude of the task of carrying through a theological revolution in the entire field. His " clue " to Christian education is that theology has been the missing element in it. Educators must become theologians, for even the writer of the simplest Christmas story for kindergarten children will go astray unless she understands the doctrine of the incarnation. And theologians must become educators. Good! But, having made this good beginning, Miller goes on at once to assume that the existing educational structure needs only to have a satisfactory theology inserted beneath it and it will be securely founded. At no point does he take account of the actual situation: that the Church's educational program already has, not only beneath it but involved in every detail of it, a number of theologies, and that, because Christian educators have failed to be critical theologians, the Church has lacked a department of theology that would help it, in its educational activities, to escape from false or confused theologies into a true theology. The problem is far too great and complicated to yield to any facile solution.

We stand, then, at the beginning of a new period of development, the period of theological recovery, and, we hope, the period in which a new unity may appear in the Church's educational program. But there is, as yet, only a scanty beginning. The work of this new period still waits for workmen. The Church has taken only a few hesitating steps. No educator of the first rank has taken the trouble to explore systematically the issues which now show themselves in increasingly sharp outline. There has been debate in abundance, but it has not yet attained the level of scholarly discussion in published works open to the examination of all. There have been curriculums produced that show clearly the marks of the new theological concern, but such productions have been severely hampered by the difficulty in finding writers and teachers who have an interest, and a thorough training, in both theology and education. Great new developments are possible, but first, the process of rethinking must be taken with far greater seriousness.

4

THE PRESENT SITUATION

IT is always much easier to describe the past than the present, for as we move away from the scene of action, it falls into clearer perspective. We are so immersed in the details of the present moment, and we ourselves are so much a part of the situation, that we have difficulty in attaining the objectivity necessary for description. Thus, what seems to one person an unhealthy overweighting of education with theological concern may be to another the most hopeful sign in the whole situation. The best that anyone can do is to portray the situation as it appears from where he stands.

THE RIGIDITY OF TRADITION

The tracing of the lines of development in the past is actually a drawing in of the background of the present. We are, in a large degree, what the past has made us. We did not choose that things should be as they are; we merely took over an order that had been established before we came upon the scene. Many of our attitudes, practices, approaches to problems, and even antipathies, in this field of education are not the result of our independent examination of facts and conscious thinking through of the problems with which they confront us, but are taken over, ready-made, either from the particular tradition in which we have been reared or from some influential teacher. In fact, one characteristic of the church school has long been the pertinacity of whatever tradition happens to become established in it, a stubborn resistance to change. All human institutions and all human beings share this characteristic, and perhaps it is necessary for stability of character, but the church school seems to have had an unusual and unhealthy degree of it. The tradition of the superintendent taking more than half of the one-hour period for "opening and closing exercises," or the tradition of the twenty-minute class, or the tradition of having a Scripture passage printed in the quarterly, persists for generations and is handed down from one age to the other as a kind of infallible order that permits no deviation. Anyone who has ever undertaken the reform of educational practices in a congregation has been made painfully aware of the rigidity of existing forms.

It is extremely interesting that this rigidity is found, not only in conservative schools whose practices are used as illustrations above, but also in liberal schools where the religious education movement has produced the leadership. Even though one of the tenets of the educators has been "complete openness toward the future," a rigid dogma has developed on the subject of what can and what cannot be done with children. A certain professor of religious education asserts that it is wrong to speak of God to a child under nine years of age, because the child has as yet no experience that corresponds to the word "God." The students write it in their notebooks and after a time proceed to retail it to their constituencies with all the authority of a careful scientific deduction from experience, although it is actually nothing more than a theological prejudice of their professor. So far as they are concerned it becomes a dogma about which they never think to ask, "Is it true?" It would be possible to distill from the words and actions of religious educators a set of dogmas which, among the initiated, dare not be questioned, and he who questions them must expect to be regarded, at least in this area of life, as little better than a heathen.

This extreme rigidity of tradition in the church school betrays an insecurity. It is a consequence of the isolation of the church school and of Christian education, the cutting of this area of the church's life apart from its context in the total life of the church. This has several aspects. Practices that have long outlived their usefulness have continued indefinitely in the church school because the Church as a whole has failed to take education seriously as one of its functions and to interest itself in providing the best possible system of education. Men and women, members of the church, who in their community demand that their children receive the benefit of every advance in educational theory, technique, literature, and equipment, will allow the church school to limp along little different from what it was a generation earlier. They have a blind spot so far as religious education is concerned, not an accidental blind spot, but one that is the direct result of a deficiency in their faith. They are not seized with the importance of a thorough Christian training for their children. They are under the delusion that nothing very much needs to be done, or perhaps it is that nothing very much can be done.

It is the isolation of Christian education within the field of theology, however, that accounts for the strange rigidity of ideas and practices in the church school. The function of theology is to be constantly exercising a critique upon the doctrines and practices that exist within the Church, holding them against the criterion of what God has shown us in his Word to be the true nature of the Church, and so enabling us to see what ought to be and what ought not to be. But the church school in both periods of its development has held itself aloof from any such theological critique, and the theologians in general have allowed it to go its own way undisturbed. The theologians have even at times given the impression that they considered the church school beneath their notice. There has been no forum of theological discussion in which those who have been working at Christian education have found *their* questions being discussed in the light of all the resources of Christian knowledge. Horace Bushnell's book in 1847 and Shelton Smith's in 1941 were courageous essays toward a theological critique of Christian education, but they stand alone in nearly two centuries of history, and each touches only one aspect of the problem. The real need is for an ongoing process, a constantly renewed critique, in which all the phenomena that appear in the field of the Church's education will be examined in the light of the essential Christian revelation, in order to discern at each point what is Christian and what is not. Only when we have a critical theology of that kind concerning itself with education are we likely to overcome the rigidity of established traditions in the church school. Church school workers will then become accustomed to having their familiar traditions set in question, both educationally and theologically, and we hope, accustomed also to setting them in question themselves. A constant process of educational and theological critique is necessary to the church school. It cannot be effectively exercised from above, but must become the personal insight of the local teacher. Since theological issues are implicit in all aspects of education, the teacher needs, in some measure, to become a theologian.

The divorce between theology and education shows itself also in the horrid and wasteful gap between education in our local church schools and education in our theological seminaries. So far have the two been apart in people's minds that it has not even occurred to them that there should be a continuous and consistent program of education leading from the one directly into the other. Both are training men and women for the ministry of the Church, some for service in a special ministry, others for the ministry that is to be exercised by every church member. For the Church to have unity in its life and work, and particularly in the relations between pastors and teachers on the one hand and the membership of the churches on the other, there must be consistency in the education received by all. For ministers and educators to be trained in one set of principles and to move in one direction, while the people are trained in a rather different set of principles and move in a rather different direction, cannot do other than divide the Church. And yet it is a fact that wide differences exist between the character of what is taught in church schools and the character of what is taught in theological seminaries. Professors of Old and New Testament claim often, not just that the Biblical education of beginners in theology is inadequate, but that they have been so grounded in false approaches to Bible study and in misinterpretations that it takes a full year for them to clear away this rubbish and to prepare the student's mind for a proper method. Rarely do students enter seminary with a consciousness that their training in the local church has provided them with a strong foundation which needs only deepening and enlarging in the seminary.

If this discontinuity and inconsistency in the educational program of the church is wasteful for the theological student, it is often disastrous for others who go on to college or university. Frequently in their local church, and also in their homes, they receive nothing except a naïve approach to the Scriptures which completely ignores all historical and literary problems. Then, in a college classroom, or in discussion with fellow students, they are suddenly confronted with facts about the Scriptures that seem to throw serious doubt upon their credibility. The shock is tremendous, and seems to them to set a question mark against all that they have been taught about the Bible and the Christian faith. They may go through months of severe strain and even feel that they have become unbelievers because of some problem that should have been clarified for them, and could have been clarified for them by an alert teacher, in their senior class at home. It seems ridiculous that a student should think the entire Christian faith in danger merely because someone has questioned whether the " whale " in The Book of Jonah is historical, suggesting that it may be allegorical; yet it has happened times without number, and will continue to happen until the same frank and honest approach is made to Scripture in the local church school as is made in the theological seminary.

EDUCATIONAL CONFUSION

It is fifty years now since the great crusade began to introduce modern educational methods into the church school. Real advances have been made. Graded curriculums have long been in use, and are gaining ground, but against stiff opposition. Some churches are still at the stage of fighting for recognition of the importance of a carefully graded program. Loyalty to Uniform Lessons dies hard, particularly in schools where shortages of teachers make the superintendent favor a program in which teachers will be interchangeable, and where the desire is to spend as little money as possible. Also, the idea has persisted that graded programs are the product of the liberal religious education movement, and so are likely to have in them an unsound theology. Leadership education schools and programs have spread the gospel of intelligent methods for all departments, and every Church has done what it can through literature. Nevertheless, it must be acknowledged that in wide areas of the church school the work that is done is on a very low educational level.

Rarely does the congregation, either as a whole or through its office-bearers, interest itself in what is happening in the church school. Sometimes the senior congregation contributes to the financing of the school. More often, the school pays all its own expenses and makes a contribution to the senior congregation. The staff of the school is expected to assume full responsibility for it, and to trouble the members of the congregation as little as possible. As a consequence, it has become a tradition in church schools that educational materials must be cheap. When a program, launched several years ago, dared to assess a cost per year of $3.50 per pupil, instead of the usual $1.00 or less per pupil, there were predictions on every hand that it would fail because of the unwillingness of schools to pay such a price! It did not fail, because congregations were awakened to their responsibility to provide materials for the church school as adequate as those in use for secular education in the community. But the widespread persistence of the demand for cheap materials floods church schools with literature of a type that creates an impression of something quite other than a seriously educational institution. The child who compares his flimsy leaflet received in church school with the substantial volumes that he uses in public school, is likely to form the conclusion that Christian education is not nearly so important as secular education.

The key to any educational program is the teacher, and the quality of the program in any school will be determined largely by the quality of the teaching staff. But the perennial problem of Christian education has been to maintain quality in the teaching staff. Tribute must be paid to the faithful, self-denying service of Christian teachers in thousands of communities, who have made an impression upon young lives that has lasted a lifetime. No criticism that we make should dim that tribute. Many of us, as we look back upon the days of our childhood and youth and try to assess the forces that counted most in the shaping of our faith, remember first, not a minister, but a teacher or several teachers in church school. They were the ones who brought Jesus Christ and his gospel close to us. They were the ones who made us feel the pressure of a Christian concern, and the necessity of a decision on matters of faith. The minister might thunder from the pulpit and strike awe into our hearts, but it was the teacher who showed us the way of faith, and helped us to take our first faltering steps along it. It would not be surprising, if a reckoning could be made, to discover that more men and women are in the ministery of the Church through the influence of teachers than through the influence of ministers. The relationship between pupil and teacher can be very intimate, and often, for the pupil, the teacher is the only person he knows who tries to do anything about his spiritual problems. The teacher may mean more to him by far than his parents, so far as his inner life is concerned. It is a position of great privilege to have access in this way to the hearts and lives of children and young people.

Yet superintendents are haunted by the problem of how to secure teachers. In some schools, teen-agers are pressed into service as teachers, with classes no more than a year or two younger than themselves. Thirty-five years ago, a superintendent pressed a quarterly into the hand of a young girl and pointed her toward a group of obstreperous twelve-year-olds, saying as he did so: "There's nothing to it. Don't be afraid. It is all there in the quarterly," and a young boy, in a class close by, for some reason never forgot the incident.

Here is a letter from the minister of a small church to his national Board of Christian Education:

"Dear Sir:

"I am writing to protest the omission of the printed Scripture passages from the last issue of the teachers' quarterlies. We down here want you to know that if you can't print the Scripture in the quarterlies, we can't use your quarterlies. Our teachers are busy men and women, and when they go to prepare a lesson for Sunday, they can't be wasting time hunting up the Scripture passages in a Bible.

"Sincerely yours."

The superintendent of a junior department, when told that teachers should spend a minimum of two hours each week in preparation, stated that her department had to have lessons that the teachers could prepare on the streetcar on the way to church.

The survey of the church school conducted by the Presbyterian Church in the U.S. in 1944–1948 (Lewis J. Sherrill, *Lift Up Your*

Eyes. A Report to the Churches on the Religious Education Restudy,
1949. John Knox Press) produced some very sobering facts about
church school staffs. The teacher in four instances out of five is a
woman. She is about forty-five years of age, the mother of two
children, has had one year in college but no teaching experience except that gained in her own church school. She was asked to teach
while still in her teens but has never had any formal course in leadership education. In preparation for class she spends less than an hour
each week, usually on Saturday night. She relies entirely upon her
Bible and quarterly and has read no book or article on the Christian
faith in the past year. She regularly arrives late at church school and
is absent about ten Sundays a year. She makes little use of modern
methods in her class but nevertheless feels that her work is a success
more often than she feels that it is a failure. She attributes her success to her thorough and regular preparation.

We are prepared now to understand the low esteem in which the
church school has come to be held, both within the Church and in
the community. A prominent columnist, when he wants to describe
anything that is extremely fatuous, and the product of superficial
thinking, calls it " Sunday School stuff." The disturbing thing is that
his audience knows exactly what he means. This explains, in part,
why it is so difficult to keep boys and girls in church school after
the age of twelve, the most important period for their education in
the Christian faith. It also explains, in part, why it is so difficult to
persuade adult Christians to undertake the work of teaching. They
have a distaste for the church school, an impression of it that makes
them unwilling to accept responsibility in it. Who is likely to be
eager to take part in an institution that has lost his respect? It
has been proved that wherever the church school is re-established as
a serious educational institution, in which teachers have the opportunity to do thorough work with children, and are given training to equip them for their task, more men and women show a
readiness to accept responsibility in its program. Making the task
more difficult may discourage those who are willing " to do their
bit for the church school " but have no intention of working hard
at it, often no real interest in education of any kind, but it makes a
new appeal to the Christian who is looking for some avenue of

Christian service in which he can serve God, not only with his hands, but with his mind.

It is perhaps unfair to the church school superintendent to belabor him for taking up so much of the hour of the school. A little investigation shows that many of the teachers want him to occupy the major portion of the hour and leave them no more than twenty minutes with their classes. They do not feel able to carry on a class for more than twenty minutes. In a large school, where the assembly period was a disgraceful hodgepodge of hymns and random remarks, the suggestion was made by an outsider, rather jokingly, that the children and young people should be sent to their classes no more than five minutes after half the number present were engaged in private conversations. That would have been at the end of twenty minutes. A gentleman who taught a boys' class, and was reputed to be a regular spellbinder as a teacher, objected at once that he would be ruined if that were done. He could go at full steam for twenty minutes, but if the bell did not ring then, he was lost, for he had nothing more to say. He had no idea of teaching as an interplay of mind in which the pupils should participate actively. It was a matter of getting a body of material ready and delivering it to the boys in such rapid-fire fashion that they were unlikely to interrupt or to stir from their seats.

In another school a class of teen-age girls openly boasted that they had got rid of three teachers in six months. They flatly defied anyone to teach them anything. When questioned why they came to church school, they answered that it was because they liked being together on Sunday morning to discuss what they had done on Saturday evening. How was it possible for them to form such an attitude toward the school of the church? An examination of the school that they attended provided a ready explanation. It was saturated in a tradition of doing anything and everything in the church school except make a serious study of the Christian faith. The opening half hour was a complete bore. Fifteen-year-old boys and girls were asked to listen to Bible stories being told in practically the same way in which they were told to six-year-olds. The impertinence and rebelliousness of the girls was their reaction to what had met them in the school, and earnest teachers, who were concerned to do a thorough job in teaching them, found themselves beating their heads against a wall that had been built up by years of inanity.

Contrasted with such schools are those that have broken with the corrupt traditions of the past and have established a totally different character for the church school, making it such that it commands the respect of teacher and pupils alike. We must not overestimate, however, how far that transformation has reached. The careful survey of conditions in the Presbyterian Church in the U.S. shows that it has gone only a very short distance. The same is equally true in other Protestant Churches. And, to complicate the situation even more, many churches which have become educationally efficient under the impetus of the religious education movement have drawn from that same movement a theological confusion that cancels out many of the fruits of their educational efficiency.

The Suffocating Fog of Moralism

Another factor in the situation which deserves mention is the prevalence of moralism through all types of church school. It takes a different form in a conservative school from what it does in a broadly liberal one, the former concentrating on individual morals and the latter most likely emphasizing the social aspects of one's duty. But both agree in regarding the conduct of the children as their main concern, and in attempting, by their teaching, to shape desirable patterns of conduct. The Bible stories are consistently used, and often twisted to make them useful, to point a moral, so that the child very early forms the impression that the Bible is a book of morals and that the men and women who appear in its pages are, with few exceptions, examples of good conduct. It would make a pathetic but hilarious volume if someone were to collect from various books of Bible stories for children, and from the millions of pages of lesson materials, all the versions and perversions of Biblical stories that have been concocted with the express purpose of pointing a moral. How zealously the Biblical characters have been whitewashed, how shamelessly the stories have been revised to conceal the sins of the persons in them, lest the morally minded children should be offended, or even misdirected, by catching a glimpse of what these men really were like! Anyone who has ever been assigned the task of reading church school lesson materials in bulk, materials from seven or eight different churches, materials reaching back as far as thirty years, can testify to the high quantity of moralizing contained in them. They are literally packed with it, platitudinous moralizing, offered on the assumption that if you tell a child what is the right thing to do, he will do it. And how deadly, how insipid, how utterly boring, this moralizing is!

It is worth inquiring why moralizing should be boring. After all, conduct is an extremely important matter. Every human being is involved day by day in problems of conduct to which he must find the solution if he is to have any satisfaction in living. Why, then, should we not be interested when someone endeavors to show us what right conduct is, and to furnish us with examples of it? I may want passionately to be good; yet if someone sits down with me and tries to tell me how to be good, instead of being interested I am impatient for him to get finished and let me go. Why should that be so?

First, there is the awareness that the source of wrong conduct lies too deep to be touched merely by a few words of good advice. The difficulty, even with the child, lies usually not in ignorance of what is the right thing to do, but in an inner inability to do the right thing. The psychologists have uncovered for us the depths of the personality in the unconscious and have shown that what happens in conduct is determined often by forces far below the surface of conscious thinking and willing. Therefore, the teacher who assumes that conduct can be reshaped merely by pointing out what is the right thing to do fails to take account of the dimension of depth in the pupils and leaves the same impression as would a doctor who gave all his attention to the surface manifestations of a disease and none to its roots below the surface.

We need also to recognize the involvement of the question of conduct with the question of truth. Even the small child, when told to do certain things, responds by asking, "Why?" Parents are sometimes impatient of that question, failing to see that the child already is reacting against a standard of conduct that has no other foundation than the parent's will and is reaching out for a standard that will be more firmly grounded in the child's own understanding of things. Behind the persistent "Why?" is the demand of the human personality for ethics to be rooted in doctrine, for the standard of conduct to be rooted in an interpretation of life that will give it meaning and support. Many parents, and many teachers as well, have the idea that an ethic can stand by itself. Parents feel that they have done their Christian duty by their children when they have passed on to them, firmly and earnestly, a Christian standard of conduct, even though they have done nothing whatsoever in the home about the question of Christian truth. It is much easier and makes a lesser demand upon one's own understanding of the Christian faith to remain on the level of morals and not to venture upon the attempt to teach one's children what the gospel is, and what Christian doctrine means for the interpretation of the whole of life. But Christian ethics divorced from the Christian gospel have no meaning. They are like flowers cut off from their roots. They may live a short time, but they are doomed to die. The Christian standard of conduct is not a natural possibility for any person; it is a supernatural possibility, to be realized only through the redemptive power of Jesus Christ working in human persons through the gospel. Therefore, to impress upon a child, or youth, or adult, his duty to fulfill the Christian standard, and to leave him ignorant of the truth of the gospel which alone makes him aware how that standard is to be fulfilled, is as absurd and exasperating as to order a man to shovel two feet of snow from a hundred feet of sidewalk and give him no shovel with which to do it. Moralism bores us because it confronts us with an impossibility. By the very nature of things, ethics are always insecure until they are firmly rooted in our understanding of truth.

The plan of Christian education devised by Ernest Ligon is most vulnerable at this point, that it fails to break out of the context of the traditional moralism of the church school. Ligon has made important contributions to Christian education, notably his demonstration that parents can be drawn into close co-operation with the church school and his application of techniques for testing the pupils' responses, drawn from his experience in psychology, by which he enables the teacher to know more definitely what is happening in the pupil's development. But Ligon's curriculum plan is actually only a refined form of the moralism from which the church school has already suffered too long. It is a program for the development in the children of specific character traits, the assumption being that when all, or nearly all, the traits are present, the child is a Christian. It is subject to all the objections that are raised against other forms of moralism in the church school. It fits only too comfortably with the inclination of parents and teachers to confine their attention to problems of moral development.

We shall have to return to this subject of moralism in the next chapter and consider its significance on a larger scale, in the life of the Church as a whole. But any description of the existing situation that failed to take account of it would be highly deficient. It lies close to the center of the whole problem we are facing.

The Unfair Burden Upon the Church School

It is not the fault of the church school that increasingly with the years it has become the Church's only agency of Christian teaching. There should in the main be three agencies: the Christian congregation in its worship and fellowship, the Christian home, and the church school with its related organizations. To these, in some communities, may be added the public school, but it lies beyond the scope of the Church. If some attention is given to interpreting to the child what happens in worship, so that in his own way he may participate, the adult service of worship may prove a valuable learning situation for him. The intimacy of the home creates a unique opportunity for Christian teaching, teaching of a kind that can be done nowhere else. And yet, these two agencies have, in the present day, become almost wholly inoperative for most children, and not just for children of non-Christian homes, but also for children of Christian homes. The estimate of the number of Christian parents who attempt to teach their children concerning the Christian faith after the children have passed beyond the stage of elementary Bible stories is rarely placed higher than ten per cent of the total. And in few churches are more then ten per cent of the children of the congregation under the age of fourteen present in the service of worship. Where the church school meets before the morning service, the worshipers frequently encounter streams of children making their way homeward, and sometimes their teachers with them. They have had their church for the day. The result is that the Christian education, even of children of church families, is made to depend entirely upon the church school. The parents feel that they have done their part when they have delivered their child, properly washed and clothed and with a nickel in his pocket for collection, at the church door. Since he has had his hour in church school, it is not regarded as essential that he should be present in the worship of the congregation. But do they grasp, and does the church as a whole grasp, that the Christian training of the child has now been made to depend entirely upon the church school, placing upon it a burden that it is unfitted to carry?

The child who attends church school regularly rarely has more than forty sessions to his credit in a year. The teaching period in most schools is no more than twenty minutes, so that in a year he receives a maximum of eight hundred minutes of teaching. It is true that quantity is not what counts most in teaching, but it is equally true that teaching a large and important subject takes time, and if the time available is seriously inadequate, the child's understanding of the subject will be seriously inadequate. Eight hundred minutes are thirteen and one third hours, roughly equivalent to less than three days' classes in public school. If a public school teacher were asked to do a year's work in English literature, or in geography, or in arithmetic, in thirteen and one third hours per year, he would declare that he was being asked to do the impossible. Within that time limit even the most expert teacher could not give a pupil a proper grounding in any important subject. But, operating with teachers who are not expert, and undertaking a subject far more extensive and significant than any that are taught in public school, the church expects in thirteen and one third hours per year to give the child or youth a sound Christian education. The subject includes the whole of the Bible, the whole of Christian history, the whole of Christian doctrine, and an understanding of the relation of the Christian faith to all things in life! And yet churches still assume that it can all be done adequately within this narrow space of time. Must we not in honesty admit that we have been expecting the church school to do the impossible? Even if we lengthen the teaching period to forty or fifty minutes, as many of the schools have already done, we have not provided sufficient opportunity. There is no way out except to recognize that all three agencies, the congregation, the home, and the church school must function in co-operation with each other, and to take the necessary steps toward bringing back to life the two that have lost their place in the education of children.

The Urgency of the Hour

This chapter has purposely painted a dark picture of the present situation, for the very good reason that the situation is dark and more dangerous to the future of the Church than most people realize. There are millions of children on this continent totally outside the church school. Someone has reckoned that they number at least 15,000,000. We need to ask ourselves what responsibility our churches have toward those millions, and what we are doing to reach them. But even more urgent is the question, What is going to happen to the larger number who are present in our church schools and who are not receiving from the Church an education in the Christian faith that is worthy of it? The amazing thing is that, in spite of the radical deficiencies of our church schools, such a large proportion of the children and young people of the community have continued to attend them. It is still " the thing that is done." Even people who do not believe in any of the doctrines of the Christian faith may continue to send their children to church school with the hope that it may have a good moral influence. They want their children to grow up into good law-abiding citizens, and to that end the church school may be useful. But what if we were to find ourselves suddenly living in a situation in which the Church should be in a state of tension with the environing society because it had begun to resist some of the dominant and most popular trends of that society? What if the Church's ideal for man should no longer fit with the nation's ideal for its citizen? What if it were to happen here, as it has happened elsewhere in our time, that the Church should be regarded as providing a teaching that unfitted children and young people for loyal citizenship? Attendance at church school would no longer be " the thing that is done."

We have an opportunity at present that could vanish almost overnight. We have millions of children and young people in our church schools, willing at least to listen to what we, as a Church, have to say to them. The clear evidence that appears from a survey of the present situation is valid basis for an indictment of the Church — congregations, ministers, parents, church boards, all alike — that we are not making use of the opportunity that is in our hands. And if we continue in our blindness to overlook our educational inadequacies, we may awaken one day to regret with bitter tears a lost opportunity.

5

THE REDEFINITION OF THE GOAL

IN the light of all that has been said thus far, we must now attempt to redefine the goal of Christian teaching. The assumption with which we begin is a simple one: that what is done in the educational program of the Church today should be a valid continuation of what was done by Jesus with his disciples, then by those disciples with the people to whom they ministered, and by the Early Church with Jews and Gentiles who found their way into it. We shall differ from Jesus and the New Testament Church in many points of detail, for our situation in the Western world in the twentieth century is very different from their situation in the Roman Empire in the first century. But the purpose of our educational activity must be the same as theirs. If we are to use the name " Christian " as an adjective with the noun " education," all that we say and do must be rooted and grounded in the gospel, in which the entire Christian movement had, and has, its origin. That proposal is very simple and seems eminently reasonable. Yet it has revolutionary implications. Followed through relentlessly, it would produce radical changes in the entire existing structure of the Church's educational program. But first and foremost it revolutionizes our conception of the goal, our understanding of what we are trying to accomplish in all that we attempt as a Church in education.

THE ORIGINAL PURPOSE OF CHRISTIAN TEACHING

What, then, was the purpose in teaching, first, of Jesus with the disciples, then of the Early Church with its converts? There seem to to be three purposes intermingled. They are three, and yet they are one, being inseparable from each other. First is the proclamation of the gospel in an intimate person to person situation — not preaching, as we ordinarily think of it, yet indistinguishable from preaching in its truest nature. We find Jesus, in a variety of ways, speaking the word of God over and over to his disciples. It was not sufficient for them merely once to hear and to respond to the call, " Repent, for the kingdom of God is at hand." It was so easy for the eyes of the spirit to grow dim and for the confidence of faith to be transmuted into a neo-Pharisaic self-confidence. And when Jesus found this happening, he called them to a fresh repentance in an abrupt and decisive fashion. We need to grasp how sharply he affronted them when, upon finding them confidently discussing who should have first place in the Kingdom, he drew a little child into the center of the group and told them that unless they changed and became like that little child in faith, they would have no part in the Kingdom of God. It was impossible for Jesus to teach the disciples or anyone else without confronting them with the reality of the Kingdom and calling them to enter in by faith and have their life in it.

Second was the necessity that the disciples should be instructed more fully in the truth of the gospel, so that they might leave behind their old inadequate understanding of God, of themselves, and of all things in their world. They had grown to adult life in a Jewish society which considered itself superior to the rest of the world in its knowledge of God, in its way of life, and in its religious institutions. Therefore, they had had stamped upon ther minds from infancy certain ideas which were not likely to be quickly removed. A good example of this is the fact that not until after the death of Jesus did the disciples give up their Jewish idea of the Messiah as one who would suddenly, by a demonstration of supernatural powers, inaugurate a universal kingdom in which Jerusalem would become the center of world government. Neither in that day nor in this do men move quickly where the deepest questions of life are concerned. Sometimes the disciples seem to us painfully slow in grasping Jesus' meaning. Their misunderstanding of what is so obvious to us makes them appear almost stupid. But we have that impression only because we are not sufficiently conscious of our own slowness in religious growth, or because we fail to take into account what a radical transition the disciples had to make from the attitudes and ideas they had absorbed from their Jewish thought-world to the mind and method of Jesus in his approach to the problems of human life.

One instance will be sufficient to illustrate this transition. Has it ever occurred to us how completely different Jesus' interpretation of the Old Testament was from that of the rabbis and from all that Jesus had heard in the synagogue and the synagogue schools? It was not just a new interpretation here and there, but a new approach to Scripture. In our own world in the past century and a half, we have seen that it may take men three or four generations to get their minds around a new approach to Scripture. Jesus had no more than three years, and perhaps only a year, with his disciples. One may well imagine that, when he was alone with them, a considerable amount of time would be taken up with teaching them how to read the Old Testament with new eyes and get at its rightful meaning. The very word " disciple " that Jesus used for them meant " learner " or " student," and their education at every stage was concerned with leading them away from their old inadequate conceptions into a new understanding of all things in their existence. Jesus was conscious that he had been able to take them only a short distance on the way, and he promised them that, when he was gone from them, they would find in the Holy Spirit his own guiding presence leading them into all truth. Their education would take time — a lifetime.

These two purposes were in turn caught up into a third: that the disciples might be trained in mind and heart to exercise just such a ministry as that of Jesus himself. They were disciples that they might become apostles. They were being educated and disciplined that, through them, the movement of God's Kingdom into the life of the world, which had begun in Jesus, might continue in them with increasing power and breadth. " Greater works than these shall ye do," Jesus had promised them — a promise that we are inclined to disregard because it lifts the destiny of the Church, in which we are members, to a plane on which we are not disposed to live. It is not modesty alone that makes us deny the continuity between the redemptive mission of Jesus and the redemptive mission of our Church.

Jesus had a strategy for the salvation of the world. First, he drew twelve men into intimate fellowship with himself, not just that he

might impart to them a new religion or a new set of religious ideas
or a new ethic, but that he might impart to them *himself,* the life
that was in him, the life that he had in oneness with God. We forget
sometimes that, for a Hebrew, " body " means the whole self, and
that when Jesus, on the last night of his life, passed bread to his
disciples and said, " This is my body; take, eat," he was saying,
" This is myself, and as you take this bread into your bodies, let it
be a symbol of a deeper act in which you are taking me into your-
selves." Paul grasped this when he said, " Christ liveth in me."
Jesus' plan for the salvation of the world was that there might be
men and women in whom he would live and, because he lived in
them, God would be alive in them in the power of his Spirit, and
God would continue through them to invade the life of the world
and to conquer it for his Kingdom.

The strategy of Jesus was to begin with twelve, then to move beyond these twelve to seventy, using the twelve to train the seventy.
That was as far as Jesus reached in his lifetime, but the line of development was not meant to stop there. From 70, the circle should
move out to 420 and from 420 to 2,520, on the principle that one
trained disciple should be able to train six others. It was assumed in
the Early Church that anyone who became a Christian had chosen
this life of discipleship and was prepared to take training for it. Jesus
had made it very plain that he did not want anyone as a follower
who was not willing to commit himself to God and to God's Kingdom with an unconditional faith. Faith in Jesus Christ was not just
the acceptance of a doctrine about him, but was a laying open of the
human soul to the incoming of God through Jesus Christ so that the
same power of God that was at work in Jesus was also at work in
the disciple. To be a Christian was therefore to participate in the
redemptive mission of Jesus Christ. This was the source of explo-
sive power in the Early Church, that each Christian was a missionary. His education was training for that task, that he might be an
effective witness to the gospel in a world that, whether it was Jewish
or Gentile, was in antagonism to the Christian faith. All were not
apostles. All were not endowed with the special gifts of preachers
and teachers. But all had a ministry or priesthood and were expected, as opportunity offered, to be witnesses to their faith before

an unbelieving world. In the face of opposition and contradiction they would be called to give a good account of the faith that was in them.

IMPLICATIONS OF THE DOCTRINE OF THE TRINITY

It is clear, then, that the original purpose of Christian education can be understood only against the background of what the New Testament means by "God" and by "Church." Apart from the doctrine of the Trinity and the doctrine of the Church, which is the outcome of the doctrine of the Trinity, the New Testament developments do not make sense. The Christian Church came into being as a consequence of an inbreaking of God upon our world that took place in Jesus Christ. It was not to be described in any language that man had hitherto used, because it was a new knowledge of God, and it was a new creation and a new humanity that were born of that knowledge. When men tried to put in human words what they now knew of God and how they knew him, they had to speak of Father, Son, and Holy Spirit.

At Caesarea Philippi, when Simon Peter confessed his faith in Jesus as the Christ, the Son of the living God, the Trinity was implicit in his confession. He was acknowledging that it was none other than God himself who had met him, spoken his Word to him, and captured him for his Kingdom. It was God the Father, the Creator of the world, the Redeemer of Israel, the Lord of history, and none other, who had come to him in Jesus. This also is the content of Jesus' words to Peter, "The Father in heaven himself hath revealed it unto thee." The Revealer was God, and he who was revealed to Peter was God, the Son of God. But the final issue of Peter's faith was that the Spirit of God that dwelt wholly in Jesus should come to dwell also in him and to empower him for a mission that would be the continuation of the mission of Jesus. Thus Peter's simple response to Jesus as the Christ had implicit in it the doctrine of God, which can be expressed only in the form of the Trinity. We do not know God as Peter knew him until we know him as Father, Son, and Holy Spirit.

The first article of the Trinity speaks to us of what God is in his eternal nature, the Father Almighty, the Creator of the heavens and earth, in whom and by whose power all things have their existence. The world is his, and they that dwell therein, whether they will have it so or not. The second article speaks to us of God's eternal action for the redemption of the world. Both in creating the world and in redeeming it he goes forth from himself in his Word. It cannot be his Word, however, except he himself be wholly in it, and yet his Word must enter into the sinful human world to be heard by human ears and spoken from human lips. It must become flesh. But because the Word is inseparable from God himself, it cannot be received by men without their receiving God into themselves as Spirit. The prophets knew this, for, when they heard the word of the Lord, it was never merely a word about the Lord or a word from the Lord, but rather, a Word in which the Lord himself confronted them as a living presence before whom man could only bow in faith and obedience. The Word of God and the Spirit of God are thus inseparable. He who became the servant of the Word had the Spirit of the Lord dwelling in him (Isa. 61:1). For him to speak God's Word, God himself had to be speaking through him to men. The Spirit is therefore that form of God's nature in which he is able to indwell the human creature. God comes to man and speaks to man in his Word. But for him to be heard in his Word and for man to respond to him in his Word, God must himself come into the secret place of man's being and make his dwelling place there, in the power of his Spirit.

The Trinity, therefore, is a description of how God comes to man, to sinful man, and yet remains the God that he is. He comes in a Word, not in an act of compulsive power, but in a Word which is personal address and leaves man free to say, " Yes," or, " No." That Word was spoken by the prophets, but in the fullness of time it came even closer to us and became flesh of our flesh. The Word was incarnate in Jesus Christ. The Word became a person, a human person like ourselves, sharing our temptations and our distresses, and yet remaining God's Word, in which God himself dwelt wholly. Jesus was the Son of the Father, filled with his Spirit, the perfect revelation of his Word, and therefore able to send forth his Word and his Spirit into the hearts of men. To become a Christian was to hear and respond to the Word and to receive, or to be born of, the Spirit. God's coming to men, thus, was not rightly fulfilled until he took possession of them in the power of his Spirit at Pentecost.

It is not difficult to see that the New Testament doctrine of the Church is the necessary outcome of the doctrine of the Trinity. God's coming to man in Jesus Christ is fulfilled only when he takes such complete possession of the believers in the power of his Spirit that the likeness of Jesus is formed in them. They are fashioned into a fellowship that is wholly at God's disposal and offers itself as a body to Jesus Christ to be used by him in the fulfillment of his redemptive purpose. That which brings a man into the Church is not some belief in addition to his belief in God. If he has responded in faith to Jesus Christ, in him has come to know God as his Heavenly Father, and has received the Spirit of the Father and of the Son to dwell in his heart by faith and to rule him in all things, then he is by this faith made a member of the body of Christ and is already within the Church. The Church is the human fellowship that comes into being when God binds men to himself in Christ and so binds them to each other. The strength of their binding is the strength of God himself dwelling in them in his truth and love and in the power of his Spirit. They are in the Church because he has called them into it. And their destiny as a Church is to be the human instrumentality through which God will carry forward the redemptive purpose that he has revealed in Jesus Christ.

The doctrine of justification by faith alone should also be set alongside the doctrine of the Church as equally important for us in redefining the goal of Christian education. Behind the widely prevalent moralism of the church school lies a doctrine of justification by ethical achievement. We are to be saved by our good characters, and the development of good character is largely in our own hands and in the hands of our parents and teachers. The Pauline doctrine of justification by faith alone, which was so all-important to Luther, merely emphasizes one aspect of the doctrine of the Trinity. Whatever a man may be able to achieve in religion and morality by the use of his own unaided powers of mind and heart and will, it cannot be *this* faith in God as Father, Son, and Holy Spirit. God is known in the fullness of his being only where the sacrificial work of Christ lays open the entire life of a man unconditionally to God. It is all of God. The new life that a man then begins to live is God's gift to him in each moment. It is his only in God. He could never have achieved it in any other way. What it means to be a Christian is thus defined by the uniquely Christian faith in God. High moral achievements and noble religious ideas are possible outside the Christian faith. We ought not to forget that the Pharisees of Jesus' day attained a high level of character, and had intelligent views on many religious subjects. That which makes a man a Christian is something more and something different, an act of God's grace, whereby in the life, death, and resurrection of Jesus Christ, he makes perfect our redemption, laying open to us a new relationship with himself and with our fellow man, a new understanding of our entire existence and a new life.

The insistence upon faith alone is therefore an insistence merely that no one can be a Christian without knowing God as he is revealed in the New Testament. Moralism, in every shape and form in which it has ever appeared, is an attempt to evade the total claim upon man that God makes in the gospel. Faith is the response of a man's whole being to God as he comes to him in the gospel. To believe in Jesus Christ is to acknowledge him as Lord over the whole of life. To receive the Holy Spirit is to surrender the place of rule at the center of our lives to God. God asks to be sovereign and, where his sovereignty is rejected, he withdraws his grace. But man has ever tried to find some way around this radical claim of God upon him. He has devised for himself forms of religion and codes of ethics by means of which he has tried to gain assurance that he can be right with God without going so far as the New Testament gospel demands. If he is good enough, then surely God will look with favor upon him. If he believes all the right doctrines, then surely he can count on God's approval. If he is meticulous in his observance of religious ritual, then surely God will not be unreasonable with him about other things. Or, to put it in terms that come closest to us, we find it incredible that God should be dissatisfied with a man of good character or that he should expect anything more of us than good character. That he expects of us faith means that he expects of us a response that takes in our entire existence and in which we put ourselves unconditionally at God's disposal to be used by him in the fulfillment of his redemptive purpose for the world.

This is the faith that is basic in all that we do in Christian education. It may seem remote at first from the problem under consideration, the restatement of the educational goal, but it is remote only in the way that the footings of a building are remote from its main girders. Only on this foundation can the structure of education be securely reared. But before we can proceed to positive construction, we must examine the statement of goal that, at present, is most widely held, together with its theological presuppositions.

The Goal of Character Development

The definition of goal that has been heard most frequently for several generations, is "the making of Christian character," and among most educators there would be agreement that this is, on the whole, the most satisfactory formulation of their purpose. Sometimes it is given a more modern sound by calling it "the development of Christian personalities." In the local church school the teacher might express it more simply by saying that she is trying to make good boys and girls, good Christian boys and girls. Ask the average parent what he expects the church school to do for his children, and again you are likely to hear this word "good"; he hopes that it will help them to be good, and by this he means not so much a positive, active, aggressive goodness, as freedom from the more obvious ruinous evils that bring great unhappiness to individuals and families. Most parents would be apprehensive, certainly puzzled, and perhaps shocked, if they learned that the church school planned to make active Christian disciples out of their children. Christian character is a fine thing, but Christian discipleship is likely to mean taking religion too seriously and carrying it too far.

Before we can get anywhere in reshaping education in the Church, we must bring clearly into the open the total inadequacy of this statement of goal. It is not easy to do, for it is hard for most people to understand how anything can be wrong with trying to make people good Christians. After all, what other way is there to Christianize the world than just to keep on making more and more people good Christians? And the time to start is when they are young. Is it not perverse, then, to suggest as we do, that the misdirection of the educational movement in the church has been largely the result of a false definition of the goal? Would it not be more reasonable to say that it is good so far as it goes, but that it does not go far enough, and to add merely that we must balance character education with an emphasis upon Christian doctrine? Before we try any such patchwork, let us go to the root of the matter and be sure that we understand what has been wrong with our concentration upon character education.

It may help us to see the problem in better perspective if we go back twenty-five years in the history of the Church and set the present situation against the background of the immediate past. In the middle years of the 1920's the mood of the Church was one of optimism. It was customary then to speak of most of our Western nations as Christian nations. England was a Christian nation. Canada and the United States were Christian countries. France and Germany were Christian countries. Far away across the seas were unchristian countries, pagan lands, to which we who had enjoyed the privilege of life in Christian lands must send missionaries. But soon they too would be Christian. Nothing could resist the onward march of enlightenment. The Christian religion and Western civilization, hand in hand, were sweeping over the face of the earth, leaving men and nations transformed in their train. The outlook was most promising. Perhaps the goal would be reached within our generation. We were a Christian Church in a Christian, or at least a semi-Christian, world. The Kingdom of God was just over the top of the next hill. Student conferences displayed banners saying, " The evangelization of the world in this generation," and to almost everyone it seemed quite possible.

Today that optimism is rarely to be found among thoughtful Christians. Here and there a churchman is heard still speaking the language of twenty-five years ago and using the slogans of that day, but they no longer have power to rouse or to convince. They have a hollow sound. And with good reason. It was not the Kingdom of God that was just beyond the top of the hill; instead, it was the horror of Belsen and Sachsenhausen. In one of our so-called Christian nations of the West, the home of the Reformation, there suddenly emerged a paganism that could, with a good conscience, send 6,000,000 Jews to their death, and that threatened Christianity with extermination. The world did not suddenly become a different place from what it was a generation before. A Christian world did not suddenly become pagan. All that happened was that the world of unbelief, which had been there all along and had shown its nature in less conspicuous ways, suddenly threw off the cloak of politeness toward the Christian Church and Christian standards of life, and asserted itself as the God-hating, God-denying world that it is.

The surprising thing is that we Christians, who in the gospel have had sufficient warning of the nature of the world and of its inevitable antagonism to God and to any Church that puts itself wholly at the service of God, should have forgotten what the world has in its heart. Not only in Germany, but in every land, the world is the world. We have had sufficient illustrations in Church history of how the world, even a most cultured world, may react in fury against a Church of Jesus Christ. But somehow, in our confidence in human progress, we became victims of the delusion that in our enlightened Western lands the beast of the abyss had lost all his teeth and become a tractable, domesticated animal. Events in more than one land brought us rudely to our senses and made us aware that the world, in which the Church has to make its way, is still a world that in its unbelief stands opposed to the gospel and that, at any moment, may throw off its superficial cloak of courtesy toward Christianity and may challenge the right of the Church to continue. We are not nearly so far along in the task of evangelizing the world as we thought we were.

In 1938, Hendrik Kramer published a book whose title expresses perfectly this changed estimate of the Church's situation: "The Christian Mission in the Non-Christian World." The Church in all lands, East and West alike, is a mission in a non-Christian world. It is a minority group, not only in the total world population, but in each nation of the world — a minority that must proclaim the gospel and live out its meaning in a world for which "non-Christian" is too negative a term. Our environment, if we understand it not from its surface phenomena but from underneath, must be recognized as having in it powerful anti-Christian forces.

That the Christian Church is a minority is not difficult to see. In a world population of more than 2,000,000,000, the churches may claim a nominal adherence to Christianity of something more than 500,000,000 but this includes vast numbers whose only claim to the name is that they were taken to the Church by their parents for Baptism. In China, with its 450,000,000, a Church with 600,000 members is not likely to have any delusions about its situation. Nor in India, where there are over 7,000,000 Christians. It comes as a surprise, however, to most Christians to learn what a minority Christians are in the European countries. In France, in a population of 40,000,000 there are 6,000,000 Roman Catholics, and 500,000 Protestants. Not by any means all of these are active in the practice of their religion, but they have not cut their connection with the Church. But 33,500,000 Frenchmen are totally outside the Church. In England the situation is not much better, but of course the percentage of Protestants is reversed, so that we do not immediately recognize the similarity. In a population of 44,000,000, not more than 8,000,000 have any living connection with the Church, which leaves 36,000,000 outside the Church. In both France and England it is possible for a person to grow to adult life in a social environment that is totally divorced from the Church and in which nothing whatever is heard of the Christian gospel.

Church members in the United States and Canada, upon hearing such facts, are likely to be encouraged in a complacency about their situation. More than 80,000,000 of the 160,000,000 people of the United States are members of some Christian church. In Canada the percentage is somewhat less. Not all of these millions are faithful attenders or supporters of the church, but that is no different in the European countries. Europeans, coming to America, are at once impressed by the number of people in each community that take an interest in the Church. They are amazed when they learn the amount of money contributed to the churches in free-will offerings. Whereas, in large sections of European society, churchgoing is distinctly "the thing that is not done," it is still true in most of our North American communities that churchgoing, or at least the attendance of children at church school, is "the thing that is done."

The examination of figures for church membership and church finances seems to show the Church in our midst to be in a healthy, flourishing, successful condition.

We may be, at one and the same time, thankful for this opportunity which we still have in our communities and yet distrustful of external appearances. Numbers are deceptive. The strength of a Church lies, not in the magnitude of its membership or in the extent of its financial resources, but rather in the measure in which it is fulfilling its nature and destiny as the Church of Jesus Christ. The question to be asked in comparing American and European churches is not, Are we outwardly more successful than they are? but rather, Are we more truly the Church we are meant to be than they are? Do our churches possess a greater integrity and clarity and convincing power in their gospel and in the witness of their life than do the European churches? To these latter questions we are not likely to return a hasty, confident answer. Nor, on this level, are we likely to feel ourselves superior. In fact, the more closely we compare the *inner* life of the churches in Europe and America, the more we are impressed with the similarity of problems, weaknesses, dilemmas, and attempted solutions. Our Western world is all of a piece and the forces at work in one part of it may be counted on to be at work in some way in every other part. Surface differences conceal a profound mutual involvement beneath the surface. Both culturally and religiously Europe and America draw their life from the same sources. This becomes evident in even the most hasty survey of the history of ideas or of the history of theology. Movements in European thought and life eventually have their counterparts in America, not as imitations of the European, but as expressions of the same forces at work. Often in the past the wave of development has taken from twenty to thirty years to pass from Europe to America. This has been particularly true of theological influences for the last four hundred years, and one has only to examine the literature of Old and New Testament studies for the last thirty years to see how the revival of theological interest has followed this pattern, beginning in Europe, passing to the British Isles, and then spreading to America.

There are few phenomena in the inner life of European churches for which there is no parallel in our churches. The same points of view are to be found in both, the same confusions, the same theological problems. In Germany, in the 1930's, many church members, ministers, and theologians were carried, by their enthusiasm for a rebirth of the German nation under Hitler, into a confused mixture of Christianity and nationalism. By their confusion they shattered the Church and robbed it of its power to restrain and withstand the barbarities of Nazism. But who in America can fail to see, and to tremble at seeing, a blatant identification of Christianity with the American way of life, and a blending of the Church with an American form of nationalism, which is little different from what happened in Germany? Not many years ago, at a great convention of Sunday School workers, three different speakers made passionate appeals for the churches to band themselves together to fight Communism and to defend the American way of life. To them it was axiomatic that the American way of life and Christianity are identical. A Church does not withstand the peril of this kind of confusion merely by having more members and more money. An outstanding European churchman, after visiting some months in America, made the remark: "Your Church's outward successfulness frightens me. It is going to be so hard for you to realize, before it is too late, that at heart your Church is as sick and confused and in danger of betraying its destiny as the European has been."

Before putting confidence in our numbers, we need to ask, How many of them would stay by the Church if church membership and church attendance were no longer respectable, but rather were likely to expose one to scorn and discrimination in the community? How many of the 50 per cent of the population who are registered as church members are Christians by conviction, knowing the difference between the Christian faith and the idealistic codes of successful living which pass as Christian in our society? There is no reason for complacency in the existing situation. The Church in America, like the Church in Europe, is a minority in a non-Christian world.

If we examine with care the non-Christian world outside the Church in America, our complacency will be rudely shattered. Behind a polite exterior are concealed forces of a powerful nature that are hostile to the continuance of the Christian Church. Because they are not yet of such a nature that they openly attack the Church, they are likely to pass unnoticed. We are made aware of them as a constant subtle pressure exerting itself through multiple channels — through literature, radio, education, social contacts, political movements. It is not that anyone deliberately tries to break down our faith, but that their sincere unbelief, expressing itself inevitably in their words and actions, constitutes a challenge to what we ourselves believe. We may as well make up our minds that living in a modern world means living exposed to the acids of unbelief. What makes the challenge inescapable is that so many persons of intellectual distinction, whose influence is out of all proportion to their numbers, have felt compelled by intellectual honesty to abandon the Christian faith, and those whose minds are shaped by them are among the most vocal members of the community.

It gives a Christian a healthy shock to find John Dewey, in his little book *A Common Faith,* asserting both the urgency that modern man should find a tenable religious faith and the necessity that Christianity should be relegated to the limbo that contains the castoff superstitions of the human race. Julian Huxley, in his *Religion Without Revelation,* expressed a similar conviction: Man cannot live without a religion; Christian doctrines and practices, based upon belief in a supernatural deity, are nonsense to any intelligent modern man; therefore a humanistic faith must be devised to replace Christianity. Harold Laski, in his *Faith, Reason and Civilisation,* after sketching the achievement of Christianity in rescuing the civilization of the ancient world from despair and infusing it with new life, points out the need of contemporary civilization for a similar rescue and infusion. " Our scheme of values seems to have broken down." " I do not think anyone can examine with care our contemporary situation without being constantly reminded that we again require some faith that will revitalize the human mind " (page 28). But all supernaturalism is unacceptable to modern man. Therefore he must look elsewhere than in Christianity for his salvation. Laski finds in Communism the new faith that must be man's hope. " The basic idea of the Russian Revolution satisfies the conditions any new system of values must satisfy if it is to fill the void left by the wholesale decay of the old " (page 44).

These three examples merely indicate what the rigid rationalism of a science-dominated world has been doing to men of the greatest intellectual integrity the world over. They are not satisfied to be without a religion, and what they turn to is a purely rationalist humanism or a purely rationalist Communism. Or, if these are unacceptable, they may turn to a completely irrational nationalism. But it makes little difference whether they are rational or irrational; these religions, sooner or later, are forced to show their real nature as interpretations of human life that are antagonistic to the Christian faith. How far a humanism that excludes the Christian faith in God has spread through the American community, and even through many parts of the Church, is a question worth considering. A survey several years ago in one denomination in the Chicago area showed a surprising number of ministers who no longer believed in a personal God. How else, then, can we describe the situation of the Church in America than by saying that it is a minority that must make its way in a non-Christian world, and that this world shows itself at many points to be a definitely anti-Christian world?

It is not sufficient in this situation for the Church to defend itself against the forces that challenge it. We must ask, not, " How can we survive? " but rather, " How can we, as the Church of Jesus Christ, invade the world of unbelief that is at our doors and convert the unbelievers, even the most cultured of them, to the Christian faith? " Perhaps now we begin to realize what is wrong with an education that aims only at the making of Christian character. One does not convert a convinced agnostic Humanist or a convinced atheistic Communist to the Christian faith merely by confronting him with a number of people of unimpeachable Christian character. The missionary situation of the Church in the twentieth century calls for a Church in which each member, as he comes up against the unbelieving world, will be able to bear effective witness to his faith, both in word and in action. It requires Christian congregations in our communities that know they have a battle on their hands for the souls of men and are equipped to move into the community and find opportunities for bringing the Christian gospel to bear upon the paralyzing unbelief of men and women. But surely we must confess that

that is what most congregations are unable to do, and that the typical Christian of our time, however noble his character is, is unable to speak one intelligent word on behalf of his faith.

In humiliation we must confess that we are not ready for the missionary situation that is upon us. The word "missions" denotes an activity sponsored by us in non-Christian lands, or in distant parts of our own lands, or in underprivileged sections of our city, and not the occupation of ordinary church members. Our churches "have" missions, but they are not themselves missions. The minister of a rapidly growing church in the Far West complained, "I cannot get my people to stop thinking of our congregation as a mission and to start thinking of it as a church." He was going in the wrong direction. The real problem is to get the people in our churches to think of the Church as a mission and of themselves as missionaries. The tragedy is that, in most people's minds, church membership does not commit them in any way to personal involvement in the mission of Jesus Christ. Some people in the church may have a special vocation to undertake mission work, but most prefer to be what is called "ordinary Christians." Ordinary Christians accept the basic beliefs of Christianity as true, attend worship, contribute to the Church, send their children to church school, live decent personal lives, and support the various charitable projects of the community. They are agreed by all to be "good Christians" and are usually confident of it themselves. But nowhere in their Christianity is there any necessary ministry of faith to others, in fact, not even to their own children. They fulfill their duty by being persons of good Christian character, and it is unthinkable to them that anyone should question their credentials, either in this life or in the next.

Unthinkable as it is, we must set an emphatic question mark against this conception of the "ordinary Christian." By what authority is Jesus' definition of discipleship and the whole New Testament definition of the Church ignored? Jesus did not invite men to be good characters and supporters of a religious institution, but rather to embark with him on a mission for the redemption of the world. Those who shrank from wholehearted participation in his mission he turned away, even though they were enthusiastic about his teaching and admirers of his person. Every believer had a ministry, a priesthood, to discharge in relation to his fellow men, and therein lay the evangelizing power of the Early Church which made it able to conquer an Empire. The Roman Church abandoned this doctrine of the priesthood of all believers, and to this day maintains two levels of Christians, those with a special vocation, in whom the Church has its essence, and ordinary believers, who are not expected to have a ministry, in fact, are excluded from any exercise of the priestly office except in cases of emergency. The Reformers condemned this error and reinstated the doctrine of the priesthood of all believers, and most Protestants would vigorously defend the formal doctrine, under the impression that only Roman Catholics have repudiated it. Yet these same Protestants affirm the doctrine of the "ordinary Christian," which is a direct repudiation of the priesthood of all believers. Moreover, a Christian education that aims only at the making of Christian character is the education provided by these Protestants to insure that their offspring will grow up to be good "ordinary Christians." In short, it is geared to the production of the non-evangelizing, incoherent type of Christian, who is already the standard type in most churches.

Such extreme statements need validation. The charge is that we have had an educational system in the Church of which the deliberate aim has been to produce a type of Christian who will be almost certain to find himself helpless in the face of a world that denies the Christian faith. We have only to ask how many young people who have been in our church schools for fifteen years are equipped to speak convincingly concerning the Christian faith to young people whose outlook upon life is something other than Christian. Bring a young Humanist to the meeting of the church session, or a young Communist to the monthly meeting of the women's missionary society, and how adequately are our church leaders likely to deal with the missionary situation in which they would then find themselves? Let a man who is devoid of faith and in despair with life approach an "ordinary Christian" and what is he likely to learn concerning the resources that are available to him in the Christian faith? The answer of the "ordinary Christian" will be that *he has not been trained for that kind of task*. That is true, and that is the indictment that must be leveled at the old statement of goal.

It belongs in a setting in which the Christian ordinarily had no expectation of discharging a mission toward unbelievers. Why should he, when he already lived in a Christian nation and a Christian world?

Education that aims only at character development is education for a nonevangelizing Church. It is startling to realize how completely many churches live within walls that insulate them from the surrounding world of unbelief. One can live within the walls for years and hardly be aware of another world close by outside. An analysis of a " successful church " may be illuminating. With 1,200 members on its roll, it has congregations of 600 each Sunday morning, 300 on Sunday evening, and a multitude of organizations that are active all year long. It finishes each year with a substantial balance financially after taking care of all its obligations. In a normal year it receives about 80 persons into its membership. It has upon it all the marks of success. But a religious census has shown the city to have at least 15,000 people in it who have no active interest in any Christian Church. How many of these 15,000 did this congregation reach each year? Of the 80 members received, 40 had already been members of churches elsewhere and merely presented their certificates. Of the remaining 40, 37 were children and young people who had grown up in the families of the congregation. A congregation of 1,200 Christians, at the end of a year's work, had brought only 3 persons in from the world outside the Church! As an evangelizing power in the community, it was almost a total failure. It was content to live within its walls, taking care of the church families and their children, and congratulating itself if it could manage to " hold " them so that the world outside did not win them away. The idea that the church should have as its primary purpose the evangelizing of that populous world of unbelief at its very door was rarely present in the minds of the members, and was perhaps not even grasped clearly by the minister. It kept him so busy looking after those he had already that he had little time to think of that world outside. Surely that is the portrait of a church that has lost its mission, and that, no matter how often it names the name of Jesus, has actually forgotten the Lord to whom it belongs. And certainly an education that aimed no farther than the making of good Christians was not likely to break through that order and bring into being a Church that would be able to invade the world of unbelief and bear forceful witness in the midst of it to the truth of the Christian gospel.

It is hard for most men today to grasp that one may be a good man, even a religious man, and yet not a Christian. Being a Christian in the New Testament means an unconditional faith in Jesus Christ in which one's entire existence comes under the sovereignty of God, so that, on the one hand, one knows himself a child of God, facing life, not alone, but in the strength of the Father; and, on the other hand, one is completely at God's disposal to be used by him in his redemptive purpose for the world in whatever way he may choose. But God's control of the Christian's life is exercised, not from above, but from within, his Spirit dwelling in the believer's heart so that his life has its living center in God. The believer, however, is not alone and cannot be alone in this faith, for the same God has taken possession also of other lives. He is bound to his fellow believers, not by any natural alliance with them based on mutual liking, but by the fact that their lives now have a common center. All the problems of conduct appear in a new light, for all things must now be seen in the light of this central relationship with God. And the joy of life's fulfillment in God, as he is known in Christ and in the Spirit, is recognized as a joy that belongs by right to every human being. The fruit of redemption is that man becomes truly man. Unredeemed, he is only a fragment, a distortion of what he is meant to be. Therefore, the fellowship of believers must live for the day when all men will share this faith and in it find the fulfillment of their humanity.

THE THEOLOGICAL BASIS OF MORALISM

But this is something quite different from the life and faith of the "ordinary Christian." We must inquire, then, what theology lies behind the conception of the "good Christian," since, transparently, it is some other theology than that which is found in the doctrine of the Trinity. The problem before us is that of moralism, described in brief in the last chapter, except that now we see it, not just in the church school, but in the life of the church as a whole. Moralism has persisted in the church school, not in contrast to some other tradition in the adult life of the church, but in conformity with the adult Christian's definition of what it means to be a Christian. Ministers, least of all, can point the finger accusingly at the moral platitudes of the church school teacher, for nothing has been more characteristic of the pulpit of our time than moralizing. The so-called practical sermon, which does not get too deeply entangled with Scripture and which avoids doctrinal considerations lest they should prove uninteresting to the ordinary hearer, is usually little more than an essay on moral improvement, an attempt to show good people how they may be, at some points, better than they are. A. R. Vidler, the noted Anglican theologian, when asked to comment on the American church after a visit of six months in our midst, said that, with a few notable exceptions, he missed the notes of judgment and mercy in our preaching, that it seemed to be pointed almost wholly at moral improvement.

There are variant forms of moralism, some more readily recognizable than others. In the New Testament we find its classic form in Jewish legalism, in which the good life was meticulously defined in a legal code. It made salvation a very practical matter, for one had only to keep the law in order to be certain of God's favor. Moralism, in all its forms, makes its appeal as a practical simplification of the religious problem. The legalism of Judaism persisted into the Christian movement in a revised form and Paul's insistence upon justification by faith alone is to be understood as a rejection, not only of his own former legalism, but also of any form of Christian legalism. The Christian life cannot be comprehended in a moral code, nor can it be lived on any basis other than an unconditional faith in which a man knows God as Father, Son, and Holy Spirit.

The commonest form of moralism today is that which expresses itself in terms of ideals. Of some preachers and teachers it could be said that if one took away the word "ideal" from them, they would be left speechless. Idealism seems to them something much more refined and spiritual than Jewish legalism. The Christian is the man of high ideals who never ceases to strive for their realization. It is peculiar, and surely a fact of moment, that the word "ideal" never occurs in the Scriptures. "Ideal" is Greek in origin, and the corresponding Biblical term is "command" or "law." The Greek cherishes the ideal of honesty. The Hebrew says, "God's command is, 'Thou shalt not steal.'" The Greek has an ideal of truthfulness. The Hebrew says, "God's command is, 'Thou shalt not bear false witness.'" Are these merely two ways of saying the same thing, so that it makes no difference which language is used? It may appear so at first sight, but the actual difference is very great. A man stands under the commandment of God and is judged by it. The commandment is God's, with the authority of God in it. The man has to say either that he has obeyed it or that he has not obeyed it. But with ideals it is not nearly so clear where a man stands. The ideals are of his own choosing and can be shaped by him. He sets them before himself and yet remains master of them. They have no authority except the authority that he gives to them. He measures himself in the light of them, and, however far short he comes of his ideal, he comforts himself with the confidence that he still holds to the ideal. There is a virtue merely in having the ideals. He expects to be judged, not according to his conduct, but according to the ideals he holds. Thus, a dangerous confusion is introduced into a man's thinking about himself and, as long as he holds fast to his ideals, it is very difficult for him to recognize in himself the bankrupt sinner who can be saved only by casting himself wholly upon the mercy of God. Beneath this surface covering of ideals is a moralism that is in essence little different from that of Judaism. It is salvation by a code of ideals and not salvation by faith.

Another form of legalism is that which makes salvation dependent upon the acceptance of a code of beliefs plus the keeping of a strict code of morals. A Christian is defined as one who not only does the right things but also believes the right doctrines. Let one item be missing from your code of beliefs or let there be one point at which your conduct offends the accepted code, and there can be no salvation for you. Because this legalism includes the Trinity in the list of beliefs on which it insists, it has the impression that it is more Christian than the other contemporary forms of legalism and moralism. Actually it is only a variant of a general type and suffers from all the defects of the type. It is equally a repudiation of the doctrine of salvation by faith alone, even though it may include that doctrine among those on which it insists. It is, in essence, a system of salvation by right doctrines and right conduct, which is something quite different from salvation by God's free gift of himself to us in Jesus Christ, a gift that can be received only by yielding ourselves to be indwelt by God in his Spirit.

The difficulty in defining the moralism that pervades the Church in different forms is that we speak of it as though it were only in others and seem to deny its presence in ourselves. But we do not understand ourselves until we know that the dilemma of our own souls arises from our involvement in it. We have grown up in it. We have breathed it in from all sides. So saturated are we with it that we are unconscious of its presence in us. It is so close to us and so much a part of our being that we cannot see it. We think we have escaped from it, only to discover afresh that we have been depending, not upon God as we know him in his Word and his Spirit, but upon our own ability to live a satisfactory moral and spiritual life. Let us ask ourselves — and let us answer honestly: In so far as we have confidence that we are accepted with God, what is the basis of our confidence? Does not the mind instinctively begin to examine the personal record of our actions and beliefs? Because we believe in God and in Jesus, because we have been faithful in the work and worship of the Church, because we have not been guilty of ruinous sins, because we have certain acts of Christian service to our credit, we have the right to count ourselves Christians. It is only reasonable. How could God do other than accept a person with such a record? But we have not yet mentioned the one question on which, for Jesus, everything depended: Have we acknowledged with honesty that we cannot live a moment without God, that of ourselves we die daily in our sin, and that we are willing, if God will forgive us our sin and be our God, to yield ourselves wholly to his sovereignty? That is faith. It means that we set our confidence, not upon the record of our actions and beliefs, which leads us inevitably into new forms of self-righteous moralism, but wholly upon God, God our Father Almighty, who redeems us in Jesus Christ and comes to dwell with us in the power of his Spirit.

We can at least see now a little of what is involved in redefining the goal of Christian education. It is not a minor adjustment affecting only the church school. The Church as a whole, and that means the total membership of the Church, is involved in the problem. The redefinition can be accomplished only by recovering our continuity with the line of development that is marked out for us in the New Testament. Our goal must be no lesser goal than that which Jesus and the apostles had before them. We teach so that through our teaching God may work in the hearts of those whom we teach to make of them disciples wholly committed to his gospel, with an understanding of it, and with a personal faith that will enable them to bear convincing witness to it in word and action in the midst of an unbelieving world. We teach so that through our teaching God may bring into being a Church whose glory will be the fullness with which God indwells it in his love and truth and power, and whose all-engrossing aim will be to serve Jesus Christ as an earthly body through which he may continue his redemption of the world. We teach young children and youths and adults that by the grace of God they may grow up into the full life and faith of his Church, and may find their life's fulfillment in being members of the very body of Christ and sharers in his mission.

6

THE SHAPING OF THE EDUCATIONAL PROGRAM

ALL that has been said thus far can be summed up in two sentences. Christian education exists because the life that came into the world in Jesus Christ demands a human channel of communication that it may reach an ever-widening circle of men, women, and children, and become their life. The aim of Christian teaching is to widen and deepen that human channel, to help forward the growth and enrichment of the human fellowship, through which Jesus Christ moves ever afresh into the life of the world to redeem mankind. The program, therefore, must be such that it will lead people, from their earliest to their latest years, ever more fully and in the most definite way into the faith and life of the Church of Jesus Christ.

THE CENTRALITY OF THE CHURCH

The Church is thus the focal point round which the educational program is built. There has been debate for years between advocates of a Bible-centered curriculum and advocates of a child-centered curriculum. Perhaps the antithesis has persisted because of the lack among educators of an understanding of the Biblical doctrine of the Church. As we saw in Chapter 2, the Bible and the Church belong together, and cannot be separated from each other. Equally true is it that the child and the Church belong together, and cannot be separated. The child is not for us an isolated child but is a child whom God has called into his Church through the word of the gospel and whose primary need is to be fed and guided spiritually, so that he may grow up to take his place fully and maturely in the

Church of Jesus Christ in our time. It is in the Church, therefore, that the antithesis between "Bible-centered" and "child-centered" is resolved. Training to become a Church of witnessing disciples requires thorough study of the Scriptures, for the Christian disciple must be armed with the sword of the Spirit which is the word of God if he is to give a good account of himself in a non-Christian world. But such education will fail if it does not, at every stage, take careful account of all the factors that enter into the development of the pupil. The Church consists of persons, and it is the growth of those persons from infancy to old age that is the concern of Christian education. But that growth is not merely in personal character or in social responsibility, but into the faith and life of the Church, which is the body of Jesus Christ. Within this larger context, it does mean in the most decisive way the growth of personal character and the awakening of social responsibility. But these are not left vague and undefined, to be assimilated to some other context, such as bourgeois society, or the labor movement, or a national way of life. It is the character and the social responsibility of the disciple who knows himself called to serve Jesus Christ in the whole of life, and who takes his starting point and standing ground within the worship and fellowship of the Church.

It has been the lack of an adequate doctrine of the Church that has let many things that belong together in Christian education fall apart. The separation of the church school from the Church, and of Christian education from Christian theology, and of education in the Scriptures from education for living, all have their origin in this lack. Liberal theology tended to define a Christian as one who held to a certain body of liberal ideas and governed his conduct by those ideas, his relationship to the Church being a secondary matter, in fact, not essential to the healthy operation of his Christianity. By some liberals it was even suggested that one might serve Jesus Christ more effectively through some other channel than the Church, that the Church has become an impediment in the way of the Christian as he seeks to serve his fellow men. Fundamentalism also has tended to bypass the Church, defining the Christian as one who accepts certain fundamentalist doctrines and holds firmly to the fundamentalist way of life. Again, the relationship to the Church is a secondary matter, a practical question that belongs outside the essential and necessary core of faith. It is adherence to a point of view and not one's relationship to the Church that counts. And wherever the Church shows itself unsympathetic to the required point of view, it is to be roundly condemned as "apostate," and rejected in favor of some organization that conforms more closely to the required standard. It is this characteristic in fundamentalism that has made it a source of divisiveness in the various churches and an encouragement to its adherents to leave the Church of their origin and join one of the new denominations in which their point of view has more hearty acceptance.

We have seen, however, that in the New Testament becoming a Christian is not to be identified merely with the adoption of a particular viewpoint or the acceptance of a set of doctrines. The Christian faith results in a very definite viewpoint and has to be formulated in doctrines, but its essence is in a personal relationship between God and man. God comes to sinful man in Jesus Christ, and when man, in the nakedness and despair and hunger of his soul, receives the mercy and goodness of God in Jesus Christ, he begins life a second time, he is born anew, this time with God as the center of his being in the power of His Spirit. He is bound into a fellowship with all who share with him in this new life through Jesus Christ so that he has his life in the Church, and not just the Church of the present but the Church of all the ages. He knows himself one with the whole Church of God across all the earth and through all the centuries. The fact that there is unfaithfulness in that Church, both in the past and in the present, does not alienate him from it or make him stand apart from it as though it were an unworthy context for his faith, because he is acutely aware that there is unfaithfulness also in him. He has no choice except to have his life within the Church, for his birth of the Spirit was birth into the body of Jesus Christ, and therefore, into the fellowship of all who are of that body.

The Christian is not indifferent about doctrines of the Church, but to him they are comprehensible only as elaborations of the meaning of that central faith in God as Father, Son, and Holy Spirit, in which one becomes a Christian. To say, as Roman Catholicism and some forms of Protestantism do, that to doubt any doctrine of the Church makes impossible the salvation of a man is a perversion of doctrine. A man is saved, not by adherence to doctrines, but by the grace of God in Jesus Christ, and it is not possible for him in this life to escape wholly from unbelief, any more than it is possible for him to escape wholly from his sin. The cry of faith, recognized and honored by Jesus as a cry of genuine faith, was, " Lord, I believe; help thou my unbelief." God does not ask of us a dissimulation of our honest doubts. He does not ask us to say that we see more than we do. Rather, he asks of us honesty before him and that we do not make our uncertainties about details of Christian doctrine or of the Biblical story into excuses for withholding from him that total response of our being which is faith. The Church, of which we are a part, is at one and the same time a faithful Church and a sinful Church, a believing Church and an unbelieving Church. Were it otherwise, it would be the Church Triumphant, wholly redeemed, a Church not of men but of angels. It is in spite of our sin and unbelief that God takes us into his Church, makes us a people for his service, and carries forward his work of redemption, both in us and through us.

Escape from Abstractions

We must draw out some of the practical consequences of this doctrine of the Church which is the foundation of the entire structure of Christian education. One is struck at once by the concreteness that it gives to the whole process, in contrast to the abstractness of an education that centers upon the making of character or the teaching of a generalized Christianity. We must acknowledge that many of those whom we meet outside the Church, who own an allegiance to high ideals and to Christianity but have not the slightest sense of responsibility for the Church, were educated in that direction in our church schools. They were educated in Christianity but not into the Church. They never got beyond abstract ideals and ideas. They received a religious education that had little or nothing to do with the Church, except that it was given in a building owned by the Church. They learned nothing of the history of the Church. They received no training for participation in its worship. They experienced nothing of its fellowship beyond the hour in church school or a second hour on the basketball floor. People were terribly eager to hold them for the Church, but never confronted them with the breath-taking possibility that they might *be* the Church. And so they drifted out of reach of the Church, without ever making contact with the divine-human reality which is the Church and which, had they found their place in it, would have given a totally different meaning to their lives.

Another consequence of this education in a generalized Christianity is that, as the critical faculty sharpens in youth and they begin to see with dismay the disparity between what the Church professes to be and what it is — incidentally a disparity that is always there and always on this earth will be there — they sit in judgment upon the Church as though it were something completely apart from themselves. Even though they are members of the Church and from childhood have been a part of it, they now feel themselves to be the possessors of a Christianity so superior to that which is found in the Church that they are not sure whether they can bear to remain associated with it. But what right have they to any such lofty throne of judgment? How is it possible for them to think of themselves as Christians in detachment from the life of the Church? Why do they not begin their criticism by asking concerning the disparity between the Church *in themselves* and the Church as it was intended to be? The answer is that they have been educated in a generalized and idealized Christianity, instead of being led step by step into an ever fuller realization of what it means to be the Church. They have heard a call to have Christian characters and to hold Christian ideals rather than a call to respond in faith to Jesus Christ and to put their lives unconditionally at his disposal, so that the Spirit of God which dwelt in him may dwell in them and make of them a new earthly body through which Christ may continue his mission in the world. That is the call to be the Church, and no man who rightly hears it for himself has any inclination to sit in judgment upon the weaknesses and failures of the Church in others. He is too conscious of his own unfitness for this calling to take any superior attitude. Rather, he takes his place with humility in the sinful, imperfect Church of his day, confessing its sins as his own sins

and asking that cleansing and renewal of the Church may begin
with him.

The Whole Church Educates

It is the Church, then, that has the responsibility for education —
the whole Church, not just a few specially chosen teachers. The primary educational force, which forms the background for all else that
is said and done, is the impact of the total Church upon the lives of
children and youth. What is done in a church school, what is said
by a teacher, occurs in a context, and that is the meaning that has
already been put into the word " Christian " by those who profess to
be Christians in the community. It is utter folly for Church members to think that they have no responsibility for Christian education
because they hold no office in the church school. The teachers and
officers are merely their representatives, acting on their behalf, and
their work will be doomed to failure if their witness on behalf of the
Christian faith in the church school is contradicted by the witness
of the adult congregation in the community.

On the West Coast, early in World War II, several ministers in a
certain community, shocked at the cruel injustices that were being
done to Japanese citizens, appealed to all the churches to form a
united front and to speak and act boldly in the matter before it was
too late. Some of the Japanese had sons serving in the American
Army. The minister of one church, after consulting his leading men,
reported that it would be unwise for his congregation to participate.
They were launching a building campaign shortly and they did not
want to jeopardize their financial position by antagonizing anyone.
He recognized the seriousness of the injustices, but it was not a con-
venient time for him to speak out against them. He gained his new
church, but, by their action, he and his congregation created a context for education in his church school in which no child or youth
could rightly understand a prophet of the Old Testament, or Jesus
Christ in the New Testament, without damning his own church.

Let us take an illustration, however, that is more universally valid.
Has it ever occurred to us that one of the main difficulties in getting
children and young people to study the Bible and the Christian faith
with seriousness is that they so rarely see adult members of the

church doing so? The image of a grown-up Christian, formed in the child's mind by what he sees in the adult church round about him, is of a person who no longer has to be a student of the Scriptures. Therefore, as soon as he considers himself grown up, which may be as early as twelve, he wants to quit church school and resents being asked to study his faith. That is only for children! How can that difficulty be overcome unless the adult Christian awakens to the recognition that he is called to be a disciple and that ignorance of the essentials of his faith is irresponsibility in his calling? In a congregation of Christians who study the Bible, and Christian doctrine and the history of the Church, with the same thoroughness that a lawyer brings to the law and a doctor to his books of medicine, there is not likely to be much difficulty in securing a serious application to Christian study in the younger generation.

Education for discipleship is a lifetime concern. It can never be complete. Ministers and theologians who have spent their lives in the study of the Christian faith find themselves, even after forty or fifty years, still feeling that they have touched only the edge of the subject. The Bible alone is a sufficient area for a lifetime's exploration. It has inexhaustible depths, from which the faithful workman never finishes drawing up new treasures. Then there are the centuries of Church history, the whole area of doctrine, and the endless practical questions, so important for our present-day life, concerning the implications of the Christian faith for the twentieth century world. If the full-time Christian worker finds this subject more than he can compass in a lifetime, how is it possible for the average adult Christian to consign it to a few childhood years? The tragedy is that so many cease all serious study of their faith just as the age when their mental development and widening experience of life make possible a more vital understanding of the subject. It is as though a farmer were to work hard preparing the soil and planting his crop and cultivating it for some weeks and then were to abandon it to the weeds and thistles, not even taking the trouble to harvest it.

Why has Christian education come to be regarded so largely in the Church as an occupation for children? The first cause has been the misconception of what it means to be a Christian, to which extensive consideration has already been given. It does not require much knowledge of the Bible or doctrine or Church history to be an "ordinary" Christian, good-living, church-attending, church-contributing, but without any responsibility for communicating the Christian faith to anyone else. The church member who evades the task of a disciple feels no need for the training of a disciple. A few childhood years in the church school, to acquaint him with the elements of Christianity, and a brief sermon in Church each Sunday morning are quite sufficient for all his needs. But confront him with an unbelieving world, or just a single unbeliever, who may be one of his own children, and the bankruptcy of this type of Christianity requires no further proof.

A second factor in discouraging the continuance of Christian education beyond childhood has been the failure of the Church to provide adequately for a progress in learning in the teen-age and adult years. The fear of making the courses too difficult and so discouraging young people, and the difficulty in finding teachers who can keep pace with the intellectual development of more thoughtful youth, have tended to keep the angle of progress much lower in church school than in the public schools. When a church dares to give sixteen-year-olds a course equal in strenuousness to a fourth year high school course in history or literature, the cry at once goes up from many quarters: "You cannot expect young people of this age to work so hard in church school," or "Our teachers are complaining that it takes too much preparation to teach a course such as this." What they do not realize is that their failure to hold young people and adults in their educational program is a direct consequence of their unwillingness to take the subject matter of Christian education with sufficient seriousness.

Adult education in the local church too often consists only of a Bible class of which the procedure has remained unchanged for a half century. In many instances, as the older members disappear, the class itself drops away. There is need, in each congregation, for rethinking the approach to adults and the mapping of a program that will provide, not merely for Bible study, but for the total equipment of adult Christians to take up their mission as disciples in the community. A number of denominations in recent years have taken great strides ahead in this field. Study needs to be kept closely coordinated with action so that it is seen as the necessary background for an intelligent approach to definite problems. Provision also needs to be made for getting the better and more readable Christian books into people's hands, for many adults can accomplish more in private study than in a group. They ought never to be made to feel that unless they join the adult Bible class they are shirking their educational responsibility. On the adult level there must be a wide variety of approaches. Some who would never attend a Sunday class can be reached by a midweek course of lectures, or a midweek study and discussion group. Also, where a church has an evening service on Sunday, a minister can make it an important part of his educational program, by giving sermon-lectures on Biblical and related subjects. Fifty people may seem a small congregation for worship, but if those fifty people, during a year, are taken through a careful study of an Old Testament and a New Testament book, a period of Church history, and a discussion of some present-day problems of the Christian faith, it becomes a significant educational achievement.

The Place of the Scriptures

We must try now to see in greater detail the structure of a program of Christian education that seeks to provide for the growth of persons, in the most definite way, into the full faith and life of the Church of Jesus Christ.

First, it must be education in the Scriptures, for, apart from the Scriptures, we never rightly know what the Church is. We shall be dealing more fully in the next chapter with the question of the Scriptures in education. Here it is necessary only to show their place in the total program. The statement of goal, as we have formulated it, could be grossly misinterpreted if it were taken to mean no more than the growth of persons into the existing Church. The program would then be simply a means of securing the greatest possible measure of conformity with the Church as it is, and there would be in it no revolutionary force, no reforming power, reaching out boldly beyond the Church as it is to the Church as God intends it to be. There are churches that so understand the purpose of education and for which conformity is the ideal. This is eminently true of Romanism, but not of Romanism alone. Some Protestant churches are so unmindful of their heritage that they slip into the same groove.

The Scriptures are the surest safeguard against this misconstruction, for in them the Church of Jesus Christ stands forth ever afresh in contrast to the Church as it is. In the Scriptures of both the Old and the New Testaments, we are constantly aware of two churches: a true and a false, a Church that is responding to God in faith and obedience and a Church that is content with its own moral and religious attainments and refuses to let God have his way with it. There is a Simon Peter who confesses his faith in Christ as his Lord, and is thereby rock on which a Church can be built; but there is also a Simon Peter who denies his Lord and comes close to losing all share in the Church of his Lord. There was one Church in Jeremiah, but another in the priests of the Temple who stood opposed to him. There was one Church in Paul, a universal fellowship of believers, but another Church in the Judaizers who could not get free from their legalistic conception of religion. Education into the Church of Jesus Christ means, therefore, education into the one true universal Church, founded upon the prophets and apostles, the body of Jesus Christ himself, and revealed to us today only through the Scriptures. In so far as the existing Church fails to be that Church of Jesus Christ, our education in the Scriptures make us rebels within it, working for its reform, that it may be reshaped into its true likeness.

The unique place which the Bible holds in the curriculum corresponds to the unique function of the Bible in the Church as a whole. The church school, as one aspect of the Church, exists that men and women and children may come to know God as he has revealed himself in his Word. To know him is life, the only life that is worthy of the name, the life of God's Kingdom, life in which the darkness and misery of evil are overcome, life in which there is no death. God's chosen way of coming to us is through a Word, a word that sounded in the ears of the prophets and psalmists, in the fullness of time was incarnate in Jesus Christ, was heard and spoken by the apostles, and of which the record is preserved for us in the Scriptures. Through that record, the Word that was once heard and spoken sounds ever anew into the life of the world. The revelation of God in the Scriptures is unique; it is not one among many revelations of God which are to be set in line with each other and weighed and compared. God speaks to man through the Scriptures a word of judgment and mercy which, if it is not heard in this place, is not heard at all. Where else in all the ages of human experience is God made known as the Father Almighty, Creator of the heavens and the earth, as man's Lord and Redeemer, taking up our humanity into his divinity, and as God's own Spirit, claiming the inmost self of every man as his dwelling place. Close the Scriptures, and that God, who alone is the God of Christians, is unknown. And where he is unknown, the life that he alone gives to men through faith in him is unknown.

The Scriptures are central, then, in the curriculum, that God may make himself known through them and open to men the life of his Kingdom. They are to be studied, not for their own sake, but for the sake of the revelation of truth and life that may take place through them. Therefore, they must not be studied *by themselves alone* and divorced from the life situations of today in which the revelation of God must take place. Too often in the past the Bible has been considered in isolation, as though the mere learning of stories and texts from it, and the memorizing of passages from it, were sufficient for children at certain ages. But the Bible unrelated to life cannot be the word of God, and a child may be familiarized with much of the contents of the Bible and yet remain totally ignorant of God. The heaping up of information about what is in the Bible does not necessarily lead to a Christian knowledge of God. Therefore, the practice in curriculum of concentrating in one unit upon Biblical information and then in another unit upon life problems divorces the two elements that need to be brought together. Young people can find no Christian solution of their life problems unless, in the midst of them, they begin to hear what God has to say to them, and they can find no interest in the Bible until they discover that the word it speaks has to do with the very problems that are most urgent for them. Thus, when we say "education in the Scriptures," we mean something much wider than education in the Scriptures alone. The Bible must be related to the whole of life if it is to be rightly and fruitfully studied.

Perhaps we can link the purpose of Bible study in the curriculum still more closely to our comprehensive statement of goal. The purpose must be that children, young people, and adults may be brought into living fellowship with the prophets and apostles and with Jesus Christ himself, so that the word of God, which was alive in them and like a sharp two-edged sword as it came forth from them, may be alive and have its cutting edge in these Christians of today. It is not sufficient merely to know what Jeremiah said in a critical situation in Judah in 600 B.C.; in fellowship with Jeremiah, Christians of the twentieth century must learn to speak the same word into the critical situations of their own communities. The goal of Bible study is not the production of men and women who can tell you a host of facts about the contents of the Bible and can quote a great number of verses from it, but rather, the calling into being of persons in whom the mind and spirit, the passionate devotion to truth and justice, of the prophets and apostles will be re-created. There has been far too much pious sentimentalism and what is called the devotional approach to the study of the Bible, and not enough hard-headed, thorough delving into it, to get at the truth which it contains, in which alone our generation, or any other generation, can find the clue to the solution of the dilemmas of its existence. Bible study, as we have described it, is a dangerous occupation in which to engage. One has only to think of the situations in which prophets and apostles found themselves in their service of the word of God to recognize that he who enters upon the service of the same Word today must be prepared to find himself in the midst of a battle. But perhaps, if young people had some inkling of the dangers of real Bible study, it might have more fascination for them. They would then study it with the intensity that soldiers give to the study of their weapons when they are preparing for battle.

Worship

Secondly, Christian education on this basis must be a step by step growth into the life which the Church has with God in worship. Education into the Church is initiation into a worshiping community. Before the Church can do anything or say anything, it must have its being, and it has its being in worship, which is its humble, grateful response to God who, by his Word, has called it into being. All the Church's activities and utterances are manifestations of its being, but behind them, as their hidden source, is the Church's communion with God, the unceasing movement of God into the life of his people and the answering movement of their heart and life, responding to him in gratitude, love, and obedience. It is not only in formal worship that the Church knows the joy and the strength of that pure existence in communion with God. The bread of life that is offered in Word and sacrament in formal worship is bread for every day and every moment. The members of the Church do not cease to be the Church when they are scattered to their several occupations, and, wherever they are, they must feed continually upon the bread of life or they die. Our daily life is not life but rather death, unless, in every hour of every day, we are the Church that abides in God and has God's Word abiding in it. Worship is the Christian's vital breath.

Therefore, we must plan how the child, from earliest years, may be led into meaningful participation in worship. Here, the parent plays a very great part. The first lessons are learned in the home, and who that has listened to a child's first prayers can underestimate their importance? The prayers of little children must be a great joy to God. But the child needs guidance in order to grow in private worship and find, at each stage of development, new meaning in prayer. But equally important is the child's introduction to public worship. And yet often no help is given in understanding what is being done in the various parts of the service. Why are there different prayers, and what is a person supposed to do while the minister is praying? Why do we sing hymns? What is a benediction? Where does the money go after the ushers take it up to the front of the Church? These, and a hundred other questions, need answers, and unless the parent gives some thought to them, they are likely to remain unanswered. A certain amount can be done by the church school, but the problem is so large and constant that only the parent can give the full help needed. The child who is learning to read will follow the Scripture reading and the words of the hymns much better if the parent runs his finger along the lines to mark the place so that the child can keep his eye on the right word. It might surprise us how many adults in a congregation have never had the significance of the different parts of a service of worship explained to them and so miss much of their meaning. The parent is likely to have to study the service himself more carefully than ever before if he undertakes to explain it to his child.

Many years ago, a remark by James Rathbone Oliver, in one of his books, about worship's being an admirable learning situation for children, made a deep impression on my mind. He pointed out that there is a solid structure in congregational worship, with elements constantly varying within the structure. The child, with a little help, a little intelligent interpretation, can become, not an onlooker, but an active participant, which is much more satisfactory for the child, who loves to do things. The changing elements in the worship keep him constantly reaching out beyond what he has already grasped. People who report their children to be uninterested in worship or to have a positive distaste for it need to ask themselves whether or not this is the consequence of a parental failure to provide the necessary assistance in discovering the meaning of worship. Have they merely taken the child to church and made him sit quietly beside them, expecting him, wholly on his own, to discover how to worship intelligently and with satisfaction?

Sometimes, worship in the church school educates children, not into the worship of their church, but rather, out of it. Some church schools use hymns that in tone and content, in words and music alike, are in radical contrast to the hymns that are used in the worship of the congregation. Growing up with these hymns, children and young people become emotionally conditioned by them so that in the worship of their own church they feel ill at ease. They miss the rollicking swing of their "Sunday School hymns." In brief, the training in hymn singing that they have received in church school makes them much more at home in another type of church than their own.

Equally undesirable are the superaesthetic worship services that are sometimes concocted as substitutes for worship, and the sloppy informalities that too often characterize the opening sessions. Worship in the church school should be taken as seriously as worship in the church, and should draw upon the riches of the Church's heritage of worship. It should be planned so that it may be, in the fullest sense, education step by step to participate as completely as possible in the life which the Church has with God in worship.

FELLOWSHIP

Thirdly, Christian education must provide for a growth of the individual into the larger life that is possible in the fellowship of the Church. The word "fellowship" suggests to our minds recreation and social activities in general. Many people think of this aspect of church life as a sugar-coating for religion, an "entertainment" angle which must be added in order to hold young people, but which has little or nothing to do with the Christian faith itself. "They won't stay with you unless you give them a good time." If this were a valid understanding of fellowship, then we should have to agree with those churches which ban all social activities as being the introduction of a purely secular element into the Church. But let us go back to our definition of the Church. God in Christ not only binds men to himself and opens to them the joy of communion with himself; he also binds them to each other in love, and one of their greatest joys is in this fellowship of faith. It is different from ordinary good fellowship because of the depth of its origin; for they hold to each other, not because of their liking for each other, but because their lives henceforward have a common center in God. Their openness toward God calls for a corresponding openness toward each other. And an obstacle in the way of this fellowship on the human level, between man and man, has to be cleared quickly out of the way or it will reach up and up until it blocks the channel also between God and man.

In the New Testament, one of the most impressive indications of the power of the gospel is the way in which the hard center of self-concern in men and women was broken, and, in their new God-centeredness, they were open to each other's joys and sorrows, problems and perplexities, in a way that had never been seen on earth before. The early Christians were willing even to surrender their private possessions that the material wants of their fellow Christians might be supplied. To them, it was intolerable that one should have more than enough while others were cold and hungry. The bond between them was so strong that they were able to help each other to recognize and overcome their sins and weaknesses. But above and beyond all that, there was a sharing of life and faith that made the Christian fellowship a strength and joy to all who were in it. A child grew up, not in isolation, but in the midst of Christians who were intensely concerned about his welfare and willing to do anything in their power to forward his growth.

We have only to describe the fellowship of the Early Church to be made aware of the deficiency of the modern congregation. The intense individualism of our contemporary society has impregnated the Church. Countless church members think and act as though their religion were a purely private matter. They do not let themselves be bound to anyone in the church, or only to a small group of persons with whom they feel happy and comfortable. With most of their fellow members they go only as far as politeness demands, and often not even that far. In their secular associations, lodges, and clubs, they are much freer and warmer in their fellowship than they are in the Church. It is the shame of the Church that there are so many congregations where a stranger can enter and leave without ever being made aware of the existence of any fellowship. This is nothing less than a failure of the church to be the Church; it has become a conglomeration of individuals rather than a close-knit fellowship. It is an awareness of this failure, without any understanding of its source or remedy, that makes men import into the Church a purely secular type of back-slapping good fellowship that is really only a superficial impersonation of Christian fellowship, concealing a basic unwillingness of men to take their relationship with each other seriously. The true fellowship is one of the choicest fruits of faith; in fact, it is the community of faith, the family of God, which from the very creation God has been seeking to bring into being upon earth, and it is in this community of faith that God means each Christian to have his life. The Christian life is not possible for anyone who deliberately cuts himself off from human fellowship. The desire to be alone with no responsibility for anyone except oneself, is the very essence of godlessness. Faith involves us at every point in a two-way relationship — with God and with our fellow man. To be a Christian is to have our souls so laid open to God that we can close them to no man, not even to those who most deeply offend us.

This, then, is the fellowship into which the child must grow from the first moments of his life. The home, if it is a Christian home, receives him into the warmth and joy of this fellowship. But soon it must reach beyond the home. The nursery class has as one of its most important functions the successful bridging of the gap between the home and the church school. Some adults, hearing little of religious instruction in the nursery and seeing much that seems to be just play, begin to wonder if it has any religious significance. Let them take account of what the class is doing to guide the child's first steps outside the home into a real fellowship with other children and adults within the church. As the child progresses through the church school, each class should be regarded as a unit in the fellowship of the church, and great care should be taken to see that each child is incorporated into the common life of the group. Parties, picnics, and recreational programs should not be regarded as "come-ons" to encourage good attendance, but as opportunities outside the class sessions for members of the group to get to know each other better and to realize something of the meaning of Christian fellowship. This is particularly important in larger communities, where children in a class may see each other normally only for the one crowded hour on Sunday. But also in smaller communities there is need for children to meet on a different basis from what they do elsewhere, and, with guidance, to find a different kind of fellowship with each other from that of their usual daily contacts.

No opportunity should be lost for creating a bond between the adult congregation and the children and young people. An outing in the country where all mingle freely can serve this purpose well. A Christmas pageant at least brings the children before the eyes of the congregation. Adults need to be made aware of what a part their interest in the children and young people can play in making them feel the reality of the church fellowship. Do they take the trouble to learn the children's names, one by one? Does even the minister know the children by name? A minister who takes great care to know the names of all the adults in his congregation will often neglect to fix the names of the children in his mind. Therefore, they never feel that their existence is quite recognized by him. One has only to see a six-year-old child's face light up when a minister or other adult member of the congregation, passing on the street, calls the child by name, to know the value of a name. A few words of kindly interest spoken to a child by an adult may do more to make the child feel a part of the total church than months of formal teaching. The church should be a family, a family of faith in which the members know and understand each other, and education into the Church is growth into one's full participation in the family.

THE CHURCH OF THE AGES

Fourthly, Christian education must provide for growth, not just into the Church of today but into the Church of the ages, a Church whose depth of life and faith is revealed in history. The Church did not begin yesterday. It has nineteen hundred years of history behind it, and beyond that lie more than fifteen hundred years of history within the framework of Israel. With good reason history has a very prominent place in the Scriptures. What God is doing in any one moment is always understood in the perspective of what he has been doing through the centuries. The believer does not live on the pin point of the present moment, nor does the Church. It is a fellowship in which the ages are bound together and the prophet of a thousand years earlier, though dead, yet continues to speak. The situation of the present, whatever it may be, is to be faced with the accumulated resources of faith that are the historic heritage of God's people.

The history of the Church is its memory of itself. Ignorance of its history is equivalent to loss of memory. It will make more vivid to us what this means if we consider what memory or loss of memory entails in one person's life. Judgment is to a large extent a product of our accumulated experience which is stored in memory. In a moment, we bring to bear upon the immediate problem a lifetime's store of thought and living. We have learned by experience where certain paths lead. If we begin with a certain attitude or action, we shall end years later with a certain consequence. Even such a simple matter as finding our way home for dinner depends upon remembering what we learned in the past about the streets of our town.

The man who has lost his memory cannot even find his way home for dinner. He is unable to perform the simplest acts intelligently because he no longer has his past experience available. He has only the immediate impressions of the moment, which, divorced from their perspective with the past, are utterly confusing and incomprehensible. The plight of a Church that has forgotten its history is something like that. It has to keep making all the old mistakes over again, because the experience of the Church in the past counts for nothing. It has no perspective from which to judge the situations of the present. It can be led astray from its own truest tradition because it no longer sees clearly whence it came. It lacks the ability to discriminate between the various gospels that clamor for acceptance because it knows nothing of the Church's struggle through the centuries against false gospels.

The educational curriculums of many Protestant Churches have shown a flagrant neglect of Church history. The International Uniform Lessons have always limited their scope to the Biblical period and have helped to fix in the minds of people the idea that only the Bible should be taught in church school. No bridge is provided for the student between the close of the Biblical era and the present day. Educators in the Roman Church make no such mistake as this. In America and Britain, they provide their teen-agers with a large, competently written and well illustrated volume on Church history and see to it that they are thoroughly instructed in it. Roman Catholic young people usually know more about the Reformation, of course from a Roman angle, than Protestant young people. This is the consequence of an era in the church school in which the conviction has held sway that nothing but the Bible should be studied there. There is so little time for teaching; therefore, since the Bible is the one thing necessary, we should concentrate wholly upon it. Strangely, this must be described as a most un-Biblical point of view. The prophets in the Old Testament and the apostles in the New set a great emphasis upon history. To them, history was essential as the record of the covenant relationship between God and his people. It was in part the story of God's faithfulness to his Word, and in part the story of his people's alternating faithfulness and unfaithfulness. The purpose of God was always understood as comprehending the whole of history, past, present, and future, and it was traced through the record of the past that the believer might consciously take his stand in direct line with it in the present.

Ignorance of Church history leaves Protestants uncertain why they are Protestants. It is not surprising that many have only a negative conception of Protestantism, as a protest against the evils of Roman Catholicism, and when they meet a few charming and intelligent Roman Catholics, either members or priests, they begin to wonder whether our dividedness from them may not be just a product of human perverseness. Until they have read the story of how the New Testament gospel was forgotten in the medieval Church and of how its rediscovery forced upon men, such as Luther and Calvin, the necessity of being a different kind of Church from what they were, and resulted in their being persecuted and driven from the existing Church, they will not understand why there had to be a Protestant Church. And until they have learned that the basic principles of the Roman Church have remained essentially unchanged, they will not understand why there has still to be a Protestant Church. Young people, who know at what a price their Protestant heritage has been purchased, and with what a bloody and centuries-long struggle our forefathers established our freedom from the tyranny of Romanism, will be less inclined to enter upon marriages in which they sign away to the Roman Church all right to have their children share in that heritage.

Ignorance of Church history also leaves church members in confusion concerning the interrelationship of the various Protestant denominations. On the one hand, they are easily led into thinking that denominations are the result simply of sinful contentiousness, and that, if our ancestors had been more Christian, no divisions would ever have taken place in the Church. On the other hand, a narrowness creeps in: the members of a denomination, in their loyalty to it, come to regard it as the only true Church and look with suspicion and distaste upon most other denominations. Both attitudes are revealed as false when the story of the Church's divisions is read. Already in the first century there was a division between Paul's churches and the churches that looked exclusively to the Jerusalem council for leadership. They disagreed at essential points and went separate ways, yet they acknowledged a unity that they had in a common Lord. The Reformers, in their day, had to choose either to shatter the unity of the Western Church or to betray the truth of the gospel. The Wesleys and Whitefield, in the eighteenth century, could not turn back the tide of revival among the masses merely because the Church of England officially disapproved of the movement, and out of the revival came the Methodist Churches. It is surprising how few church members are aware that Lutheran, Reformed, and Presbyterian Churches were never rivals in the days of their origin, but were sister Churches of the Reformation: Lutheran Churches in Germany and Scandinavia; Reformed in Switzerland, France, Holland, Western Germany, and other parts of central Europe; and Presbyterian in Scotland. The Church of England has remained divided in mind whether to count itself a sister Church of the Reformation or an English continuation of the medieval Catholic Church. With the settlement of America, all these Churches were transplanted across the ocean and found themselves no longer *the* Church of a particular land, but merely one of the denominations of the Church. A right reading of history, therefore, results in a recognition, both of the richness of our denominational heritage and of the unity of all our Protestant Churches.

Education in Church history can be an important factor in making each Christian consciously a member of a world Church. The ecumenical movement thus far has remained too much on the level of world conferences, touching only the elite who have the privilege of attending such conferences. The problem has to be faced of how the local congregation can be made to consider itself a unit in the Church Universal. The place to start is with the education of children and young people, letting them see the Church in the Scriptures and the Church in history in such a way that they cannot help recognizing its unity — not that it may at some future day be one, but that it *is* one in its nature, that there can never be more than one body of Jesus Christ, one people of God, one Church. Then, within that unity, they begin to understand the part that their own Church has played, and can yet play.

The study of Church history gives Christians a different perspective in facing the problems of their own day. They begin to realize that God takes time to lead his people into the truth. The resistance of man to God is always great, and God is willing to wait for man in freedom to lay hold upon the truth and find the right way. Sometimes it has taken the Church centuries to find its way to the solution of a single problem. Luther and Calvin carried over from the Roman Catholic Church the idea that had prevailed there since the time of Constantine, that a man should be punished for wrong beliefs, and it took ages of suffering to bring Protestants to the recognition that no man is ever helped to a true faith by compulsion of any kind. The consideration of the Church's problems and dilemmas in other days helps us the better to see the problems and dilemmas of our own day and to know that we have a vast unfinished work upon our hands. It is not laid upon our shoulders to solve all the problems, but only to be faithful workmen, working at the task of our own day with all our resources at God's disposal.

In the curriculum, Church history and the Bible can never be separated. The events of Church history are incomprehensible apart from what we find in the Scriptures, for the history of the Church is the history of man's attempt in life and thought to interpret what he has found in the Scriptures. It is the most powerful and illuminating commentary on the Scriptures that has ever been written. The biography of Martin Luther, for instance, lights up in a new way the significance of the doctrine of justification by faith alone as we find it in Paul's letter to the Romans. Or the tragic story of religious nationalism in a modern nation takes on new meaning when seen against the background of Jewish nationalism in the New Testament. Thus, in the study of Church history, we are not turning aside from the Christian message to an un-Biblical and almost secular subject, but rather, at every point, we are trying to see in what way the Church's past experience enables us the better to grasp and interpret the gospel for our own day.

TRAINING TO BE THE CHURCH

Fifthly, Christian education, if it is to provide for growth into the full life of the Church, must have in it specific training *to be* the Church in the world of today. Theological students need not only their courses in Bible, doctrine, and history, but also practical training in the various aspects of their work. But church members are expected, after a few years of Bible lessons in the Church school, to find for themselves how their Christian principles may be put into practice. From young people one hears the complaint frequently that, in much of the teaching they have received, there has been no consideration whatsoever of what one should do about it now. If we are to educate children and young people for active discipleship, then we must give them guidance and training in the exercise of that discipleship.

Sometimes the approach to youth work takes on a defensive character. Leaders become anxious about holding young people for the Church in spite of the forces that draw them away, and they work out a program with that as their dominant concern. Nevin Harner's *Youth Work in the Church* has in it much valuable material, but is open to the criticism of being defensive throughout; never does it get to the point of asking how we train young people to be the Church. How widely this defensive mentality prevails in the thinking of the Church, every pastor who has wrestled with the problems of youth groups knows only too well. And yet there is good reason to believe that young people would respond more vigorously if confronted with the full, rigorous claim of Christian discipleship.

As part of their practical training, they should study the world in which they are to be Christian disciples. They need to understand, not only the Bible and Church history, but also the man of our modern world. He shows his face to us in a hundred different ways — in the events of the day, in literature, in music and art, and of course, in ourselves and the people with whom we are in daily contact. The Christian disciple is an intensive student of modern man, using everything that comes his way for his purpose, but having his basic understanding from what he knows of himself in the light that shines into the depths of his life from God's Word. If we are to invade the world with the gospel, we must know where we are going and what obstacles we are likely to meet, and we must have our preliminary training pointed specifically toward providing us with the weapons and resources for overcoming those obstacles.

7

THE BIBLE IN THE CURRICULUM

THROUGHOUT the nineteenth century, and widely also in the present century, the Bible has been central in the church school and often its sole concern, so much so in some quarters that it has been called a Bible school. For the past half century there has been a reaction against this exclusive engrossment in the Bible, particularly where representatives of the religious education movement have been influential, and the Bible has, in some programs, become merely one element in a comprehensive plan for the religious development of children and young people. Curiously, children trained under the second type of program, in which the Bible is not central, often come away with a better knowledge of the Bible than those who have been permitted to study nothing but the Bible. The outcome depends, not upon the quantity of time that is spent in Bible study, but upon the quality of the approach.

Within both types of school may be found a wide variety of approaches to the Bible. Among those who maintain the traditional concentration of the church school on Bible study will be found some who hold to the severest form of literalism, which insists upon the infallibility of every word of Scripture and rejects the results of historical-critical scholarship, but there will be others who, while they are convinced that the Bible is the one essential subject of study, are agreed that each part of it must be seen in its appropriate historical setting. Among those who remove the Bible from its central place, the viewpoints range from those who remove it only because they are convinced that its word of revelation will sound with greater authority if heard in a larger context, to others who believe that there are sources of religious knowledge equally important with the Bible, and yet farther afield to others who can be described as hostile to the continuation of the authority of the Bible in the field of modern religious development. We must recognize from the outset, therefore, that there is no standard approach to the Bible that a person may expect to find wherever he turns in the church school of today, nor are there simple alternatives between which to choose. Rather, we are confronted with a problem that is highly complex and in which the strands have become badly tangled in the controversies of the past century.

The Mystery of the Closed Bible

There is perhaps no better starting point for the investigation of this problem than the puzzling fact that the church school, after a century and a half of almost exclusive concentration upon Bible study, cannot and does not claim to have produced a church that is capable of understanding and using the Bible. Even allowing for the brevity of the one hour each week and the high percentage of untrained teachers, one would expect that a person who attended church school regularly from the age of three to the age of eighteen would in fifteen years of Bible study have arrived at a fair measure of competence in the use of the Bible and in the understanding of its contents. Yet how many at eighteen could be said to possess that competence? Nothing is more difficult to find in a congregation than people who have an intelligent grasp of the Scriptures as a whole and a knowledge of how to get at their meaning, either for themselves or for anyone else. Professors of Old and New Testament in theological seminaries are constantly complaining, not just of the ignorance of the Scriptures they find in many candidates for the ministry, but of the misconceptions that have become deeply rooted in their minds during their period of development in the local church. Moreover, if we can draw any conclusions from the slight use of the Bible that is made in much of the preaching of our time, the graduates of the seminaries apparently are none too confident that their three years of special studies have overcome their ignorance and misconceptions of Scripture. How else can we explain their reluctance to make wide or thorough use of Scripture? The mystery becomes even deeper when we hear of the millions of copies of the Bible that are sold each year. The Bible consistently outsells every other book. The Revised Standard Version, in its first two years, attained a circulation of 2,600,000 copies. During the past half century, a considerable number of excellent new translations of the Bible have been published and most of them have had a large sale. Why, then, is the Bible in such a large measure the unknown book within the Church? And what has been wrong with the church school's handling of the Bible that, in spite of all that it has done, it has not succeeded in getting the Bible open in the hands of Christian people?

The first error has been in understimating the magnitude of the task. The outward appearance of the Bible is deceptive. There it sits upon my desk, no larger than any other moderate-sized book. In some editions it looks smaller than the average novel. But within its covers it compasses a vast library of books, some small, some large, and contains close to one million words. The book of Genesis alone contains fifty thousand words, which is as much as many of the books we read today. But consider also that the books of the Bible are records preserved for us from an ancient world, some of them written nearly three thousand years before our time, none of them closer to us in origin than eighteen and a half centuries. They presuppose a world vastly different from the one in which we live, different not only in external conditions but also in the furnishings of the mind. Many of the writers take for granted the familiarity of their readers with places and persons and ideas that are no longer familiar to the modern reader. They also use imagery drawn from their world which is lost upon us until we know something of what life was like in Palestine. Thus, a psalmist speaks of " abiding under the shadow of the Almighty," expecting everyone to know the unspeakable refreshment of a shadow, an experience, however, that is confined to countries such as Palestine where the midday sun bakes the moisture out of the body and escape into a shaded place brings an instantaneous sense of relief.

All ancient literature requires careful explanation and interpretation if it is to be understood. But the idea has had wide currency that anyone should be able to open the Bible and read with understanding. Because some things, fortunately the most essential things, are very simply stated, and are recognized at once in their universal application regardless of the language into which they are translated, there arises the false expectation that the same should be true of everything in the Bible. The parable of the Prodigal Son speaks directly to man in every age and in every land. When the psalmist begins his prayer, "Bless the Lord, O my soul, and all that is within me, bless his holy name," there are no obstacles in the way of men of every race joining with him; he speaks a universal language of the soul. But this area in which a minimum of explanation and background is needed is not great, and wide areas of the Bible are simply incomprehensible until they are interpreted in the light of the time in which they were written and in the context of the Scriptures as a whole.

There is also the complication introduced by the fact that the Old Testament contains the Scriptures of Israel's faith before the coming of Jesus Christ, and that with the coming of Jesus, these Scriptures took on a meaning that had been seen by no one before. Paul, in II Cor. 3:13-18, speaks of a veil that hid from the eyes of the Israelites the full meaning of their own Scriptures, a veil that in Jesus Christ is taken away. The Old Testament is to be understood, therefore, in the light of the revelation of God in the gospel. Thus, when the Christian comes upon the various ritual laws of Israel in his reading of the Old Testament, he disregards them as having no application to the life of a Christian. But at once the question arises, How is he to know what passages are binding upon him and what ones are not? He wants a rule of thumb that he can apply very simply to every part of the Old Testament. But no such rule can be given him. He has to listen in faith to the words of the Old Testament for the voice that he can recognize as the voice of the same Lord whom he knows in Jesus Christ. He must read with discrimination, knowing that all parts are not of equal value to him. To read without that discrimination, as though the Old Testament in every detail were equally authoritative for Christians, is to read as though one were not a Christian but a Jew, and, if followed to its logical conclusion, that approach would lead to some such aberration as an insistence that Christians observe the dietary and ritual laws of the Jewish religion. There are some Protestant groups that have not shrunk back even from that conclusion.

A further obstacle to the uninstructed reader is the fact that the books of the Bible are not in any chronological or logical order. Genesis and Exodus make a brave beginning to the story and then the story is lost in the complexities of legal codes. Later, it is resumed, only to break off again and to be followed by a second version of the same story. Then come books of various kinds and a whole library of the prophets. The New Testament order is simpler, but even there it takes some experience for the reader to find his way about. How many thousands of young people, following up the suggestion of a church school teacher that they should read the Bible through, have got as far as the " begats " or one of the legal codes, and, bogging down completely, have failed to go any farther? And how many, starting with the New Testament, have reached the letter to the Romans and there have stuck fast? They need to be warned about the difficulties and pitfalls in the way of the Bible reader, and they need a road guide that will have clearly marked on it where they may expect to find desert country and what are the shortest routes to the places of greatest interest and profit. Above all, let them not be turned loose in the Bible with a mistaken expectation that it is quite easy to understand.

The Problems of the Scholars

If we are to penetrate the mystery of the present generation's ignorance of the Bible, or perhaps it were better called its alienation from the Bible, we need to know something of what has been happening in Biblical scholarship during the past century. At first the mystery becomes deeper when we survey the vastness of the labors of Biblical scholars in Europe and America and the hundreds of valuable books that have been produced, dealing with every aspect of the Bible and its background. Archaeologists have been digging up the past and opening new vistas for us in the history of the Near East in which the Bible has its setting. Linguists have untangled many difficult passages in the Biblical text. Historians have reconstructed for us the character of Israelite society in its various stages. Literary critics have equipped us to read, not only each book, but each part of each book in the context of its origin. These resources of learning have not been left far out of the reach of the ordinary student in scholarly tomes, but have been made available in eminently readable books, and many of the results have been incorporated in new translations of the Bible. Never in the history of the Church has so much literature been available to forward intelligent Bible study. Yet the Bible remains, for most Christians, an unexplored territory. Why is this so?

The answer seems to be that in the period directly behind us the Bible has been a casualty in a prolonged battle within the Church between opposing points of view. The Church has been divided sharply into two camps on the question of how the Bible is to be interpreted. Tragically, the book that should be one of the greatest unifying forces in Christendom has been a divisive force, setting brother against brother and creating antagonisms within denominations and within congregations which have seriously impeded the work of the Church. The persistence of the division for more than a century and the presence of earnest Christian men on both sides in the controversy should be an indication to us that each side has had a genuine Christian concern, and should make us suspect a false antithesis somewhere in the issue. On the one hand have been those who have insisted upon the importance of investigating the Bible with all the tools of modern scholarship and who have asserted that a Christian faith in God ought not to fear but rather to welcome whatever new light such investigations throw upon the text of the Bible. God cannot be injured by truth, and the slightest suggestion that the Church is unwilling to face all the truth about its Bible is likely to destroy the confidence of men in the integrity of the Church. On the other hand are those who have recognized in the revelation of God in the Bible the only source of that knowledge of God that leads to salvation and who have been dismayed to see the Bible losing its authority in the minds of men and its place of centrality in the Church. To them the investigations of critical scholars seemed to bear a heavy responsibility in diminishing the Bible's authority. Therefore, in defense of the Bible they were constrained to oppose the whole modern development of scholarship.

A brief survey of a century of Bible study will show how these two genuine Christian concerns have reacted upon each other to create a false antithesis. The awakened reason of man in the eighteenth century began to ask questions about the Bible that the Church could not afford to leave unanswered. The restless mind of man was probing into the past, investigating ancient literatures and trying to bring to life the story of the past. The scientific method, having proved itself a key to many problems, was now being used to unlock the cupboards of history. It was inevitable that sooner or later it would be applied to Biblical history, and it was important that it should be done by Christians and not by secular historians who might be lacking in appreciation of the material under their hands. During the first half of the nineteenth century the foundations of the new development in Biblical study were laid by Christian scholars. In most instances these were men who did not confine their interest to the Bible but were in the fullest sense Christian theologians. Eichhorn, De Wette, Ewald, Vatke, and Delitzsch are all honored names in the first period of Old Testament research on the continent of Europe and all considered themselves theologians. They published volumes on Protestant doctrine, on Church history, on New Testament interpretation. All concerned themselves with the theology of the Old Testament. The same is true of William Robertson Smith in Scotland, who appears later in the nineteenth century and shows himself a theologian imbued with a deep Christian concern. It was on behalf of the Church and for the enrichment of the Church that all these men carried through their investigations.

The new approach to the Biblical records resulted, however, in new interpretations, and it was most disturbing to the mind of the Church to find attitudes and points of view challenged that had gone unchallenged for centuries. It had long been taken for granted that Moses wrote the first five books of the Bible, though the Bible itself made no such claim. Now, scholars not only asserted that it was impossible for Moses to have written those books, but proceeded to distinguish within the existing books a number of ancient records, coming from different ages and combined by a later editor to form one book. Simple piety was shocked. It was as though the scholars had laid presumptuous hands upon the Holy of Holies. Traditional interpretations of the Bible were identified with the Bible itself by many Christians, and when these interpretations were rejected by the scholars, it seemed as though the Bible itself were being rejected and destroyed. So arose a wave of fear and antagonism toward the new scholarship. Trials for heresy were instituted against scholars. W. Robertson Smith, a deeply Christian spirit and a man of great learning, whose early writings show the promise of how he might have served his Church, was dismissed from his professorial chair at an age when most men are only graduating from seminary. In the United States, the trial of Dr. Briggs, of New York, warned other scholars of what they could expect from the Church.

The suffering of men such as Smith and Briggs had two consequences for the new movement in Biblical research. First, it made it a dangerous occupation, and so attracted to it a large number of men of real courage and intellectual ability who produced works of such value to the Church that they soon gained recognition, not only for themselves but for their principles. But a second consequence was the disowning by the Biblical scholar of theological responsibility. He defended himself against attack by asserting that he was merely applying scientific methods to the study of Biblical literature and history. It was his function to get at the facts and no more. The facts might be subject to a theological interpretation, but of themselves they were untheological. And the Biblical scientist, in order to reach a completely objective assessment of the facts, considered it necessary to divest himself of all theological presuppositions and all theological concern. The idea that such objectivity as this was possible in the examination of the Bible was taken for granted in a world that was marveling at the achievements of science in the investigation of nature. But there can be little doubt that the eagerness of Biblical scholars to be untheological was greatly spurred by the antagonism of orthodox theologians toward the historical-critical movement. How could a man be accused of heresy whose only concern was with facts and who refrained from involving himself in theological arguments?

It is impossible, however, for any man to deal with the content of records that have to do with the relationship of God and man and remain untheological. Whether consciously or unconsciously, he has to stand somewhere to make his observations; he cannot divorce himself from his own convictions on the ultimate questions of human existence or prevent them from affecting his estimate of men such as the prophets and apostles. It was inevitable, therefore, that historical-critical scholars should have some theology, and, since the dominant intellectual trend in the latter half of the nineteenth century and the first quarter of the twentieth was theological liberalism, and, moreover, since liberal theologians sprang quickly to the defense of historical-critical scholarship when it was attacked by orthodox theologians, an alliance between the two was the logical outcome. So close was the association that both critical scholars and their orthodox opponents assumed that the one could not exist without the other. In *What Is Faith?*, published in 1925, J. Gresham Machen, after a detailed demolition of theological liberalism, proving point by point its divergence from New Testament Christianity, announced triumphantly that he had disproved the validity of historical-critical scholarship with which his arguments had nothing to do! A few years ago, a Biblical scholar who found liberalism no longer tenable and became interested in a more evangelical theology was likely to be reproached by his colleagues as though he had betrayed the principles of historical-critical research. Thus the strange situation arose that scholars who were by conviction liberal in theology produced volumes on Biblical subjects in which they professed to be completely uninfluenced by their own convictions in reaching their conclusions, even though the conclusions were invariably in line with the general trend of liberal theology! A further complication of a serious nature arose from the fact that the basic assumptions of liberalism were at many points in direct antagonism to the basic assumptions of the authors of the Biblical records. It is not surprising, therefore, that Biblical science, proceeding in this direction, while it brought to light a host of facts concerning the Biblical history and literature, showed a peculiar inability to interpret the core of the Bible's meaning, and, indeed, raised serious doubts as to whether the Bible should any longer be considered a unique revelation of God.

It was not without reason, then, that toward the close of the nineteenth century, many within the Church became alarmed at such developments and protested that something was being lost without which the Church would cease to be the Church. Unfortunately, however, the protest was an undiscriminating one and linked itself with the earlier ignorant antagonism to all critical investigation of the Scriptures. Also, in attempting to defend the divine origin and authority of the Scriptures, the spokesmen of the reaction invariably insisted upon the doctrine of verbal infallibility, and anyone who applied his intelligence with freedom to the vexing problems with which the Scriptures confronted him was likely to find himself branded a modernist and an unbeliever. Thus, on the one side in the Church were those for whom the Scriptures were the living Word of God, which alone is able to make us wise unto salvation, but with this belief was associated a repudiation of man's right to use his intelligence in the investigation of the Scriptures. On the other side were those who in single-minded devotion to truth were prepared to find in the Scriptures whatever a completely open-minded examination might disclose, but with this open-mindedness was associated a theology which so generalized the conception of revelation that it was unable to understand or to find room for a unique revelation of God in Scripture. Part of the truth was to be found on each side of the antithesis. That was why the division between the two parties persisted so long in all our churches. And nothing in present theological developments is more hopeful for the future than the overcoming of this false antithesis, the emergence of a Biblical scholarship that takes the Bible in earnest as the revelation of God which it claims to be and which the Church has consistently recognized that it is.

It is not difficult to see the consequences of this false antithesis for Biblical study, both in the church school and in the Church. Neither approach has been adequate to make sense of the Bible. Tell modern men that to be Christians they must believe that the world was made in seven calendar days, that the story of Jonah and the whale is history, and that everything in the Bible must be taken as literally true, and the Bible becomes a great obstacle in the way of their faith. They find that they get on much better if they leave the Bible closed, for when they open it, they meet with problems to which their Church seems to have no solution. But it is equally true that, if these same modern men are given a most intelligent historical and critical interpretation of the Biblical records but fail any longer to hear in it a word from God sounding into the midst of their life, they will find the Bible dispensable and not quite interesting; they can do without it. Thus, the two antithetical approaches have operated to discourage men, even the most Christian men, from examining the Scriptures with care. Both bear a responsibility for the strange ignorance of the Scriptures that we find so widespread in the Church.

The lack of Biblical preaching stems from this same source. Many students come into their period of seminary training from churches where the approach to the Bible has been extremely literalistic and they have been warned against the godlessness of the " higher critics." It takes them three years to get oriented to a different approach to the Bible and some never make the transition successfully. Some get only far enough to recognize the untenableness of literalism without mastering the historical-critical approach sufficiently to use it in their own preaching and teaching. Also, the consciousness that there may be in the congregation someone who, if he hears the minister speak of " the Second Isaiah," may brand him a " modernist," discourages the minister from making too obvious use of critical results. He does not mean to suppress any important truth, but in the interests of a peaceful ministry it seems wise not to offend the literalists too severely. As a result he confines himself to a " devotional " approach to the Scriptures or preaches topical sermons with Bible texts merely for decoration. The congregation remains uninstructed in how to read the Bible with intelligence and to get at its meaning for themselves.

But historical criticism must also bear some responsibility for the decline of Biblical preaching. A Biblical science that deliberately neglected theological questions in its investigation of the Scriptures and confined itself to the linguistic, literary, and historical aspects of its subject, left untouched the very heart of Scripture, where alone the unique place that the Bible holds in the Church finds its justification. The author's own experience illustrates this criticism. After nine years of specialized studies in Old Testament, he became the pastor of a village church, but soon he was humiliated to discover that he was not yet prepared to proclaim to a congregation a message from God from the Old Testament. The point at which the

Scriptures became of interest to a Christian congregation had some-how been neglected in the years of study. He had to start at the beginning again to read the Old Testament as the record of a revela-tion of God, and, moreover, as the record of a revelation that had its center and climax in Jesus Christ. But this was now a different book, and even the historical and literary problems took on a different appearance. Theology was henceforward a primary concern and it became clear that a Biblical science that refuses to take theological questions seriously is a Biblical science that is unable to take the Biblical revelation seriously. Apparently many others were making the same discovery at the same time, for during the past twenty years there has been a growing recognition among Biblical scholars that to introduce a theological student merely to the historical and literary aspects of the Bible is to leave him incompetent to preach from the Bible; or it may even leave him in doubt whether there is anything in the Bible that requires urgently to be preached today.

In the church school both approaches have had the same conse-quences as they have had with ministers. The most characteristic feature of the church school's handling of the Bible has been timid-ity. Producers of curriculum have, in general, followed a policy of great caution in dealing with critical questions because they have had in their constituencies both literalists and nonliteralists. They did not want to offend either. Therefore, they tried to strike a course somewhere in between that would at one and the same time avoid narrow literalism and yet bear none of the recognizable marks of the historical-critical approach. The effect, however, was to accen-tuate the timidity of the church school about the Bible and to per-petuate the idea that certain very obvious problems in the Scriptures are unmentionable. The teacher, therefore, judiciously avoided any questions about the first chapters of Genesis, merely retelling the Biblical story and leaving the children to make of it what they could. But those children, as early as the age of nine, were learning in school of the hundreds of thousands of years of the world's his-tory. One nine-year-old, on the way home from school, was heard to say to a companion: "I guess what's in the Bible isn't really true. I am going to stick with the scientists." Not to give that child an understanding that Gen., chs. 1 to 3, is not authoritative history or geography or astronomy or biology but is an authoritative revelation of who God is and who we are, and how our world and humanity are related to God, is nothing less than criminal neglect. Yet, at least 90 per cent of our church schools have been guilty of that neglect through timidity. They have been afraid to deal frankly and honestly with the questions that arise inevitably in the mind of any intelligent person today in the reading of Scripture. And thereby they have left a large portion of the membership of the Church under the impression that their church has no satisfactory answers to such questions. We might be surprised to learn how many of our members have the fear that, if they were to let all their questions about Scripture out into the open, they would find themselves outside the Christian faith. The way of discretion seems to be to push such questions into the background and forget that they exist. But unfortunately that results usually in the Bible as a whole being pushed into the background.

When we survey the havoc that has been wrought by the false antithesis that has prevailed in the past, we begin to grasp how important it is for the future of the church school that a scientific approach to the Biblical records is now increasingly to be found in combination with an earnestness about the Bible as the revelation of God. The theological revolution that has taken place in the field of Old and New Testament scholarship during the past thirty years has profound implications for the rediscovery of the Bible in the preaching and teaching of the Church. The Bible has been investigated from cover to cover in the most ruthless scientific fashion for a century and a half and it has come out enhanced in its authority as the record of a revelation that is unique in our world. We need have no fear of what will happen to the Bible if we look at every part of it with open eyes. The Bible does not require our defenses of it or our apologies for it. It is quite able to take care of itself. Above all, what it needs is to be laid open before men with complete honesty that it may speak its own word in its own way. Let there be a purging of the church school, then — and of the pulpit as well — of the timidity that leaves children with the false impression that the Bible is not able to stand up against the honest questions which arise in their minds when they read it. The Bible cannot regain the confidence and interest of intelligent people until the approach of the Church and church school to it becomes characterized by a thoroughgoing openness and honesty in every detail of interpretation.

The Bible must be liberated. Or perhaps it would be truer to say that the minds of men must be liberated that they may roam through the Bible with a new freedom. It is healthful at this point to remind ourselves that our salvation depends wholly upon faith, faith which is the response of our whole being to God as he comes to us in his Word through Scripture. The Scriptures are essential to our faith, for without them we could not know God as our Father Almighty, as our Lord and Saviour in Jesus Christ, and in the life-giving power of his sovereign Spirit. But it is faith in God that saves, and not the particular viewpoint we may hold on this or that matter in Scripture. Whether or not Moses wrote the Pentateuch, whether The Book of Isaiah is the work of one, two, three, or four prophets, whether or not the disciple John wrote the Fourth Gospel, and a thousand similar questions can be considered with an open mind and a judgment given strictly according to the evidence. No man's salvation depends, even in the slightest degree, upon any such flimsy basis as the opinion he holds upon literary or historical problems in Scripture. In fact, we may put it even more strongly and say that it is a denial of the doctrine of justification by faith alone to require of men adherence to certain views on the authorship of particular books in Scripture before considering them to be Christian.

The Bible in the Church School

We must turn now to consider certain detailed problems in the use of the Bible in the church school.

Fragmentariness: The student very often finds himself, at the end of years of attendance in church school, with no grasp of the Bible as a whole and no ability to find his way in it. It has been presented to him in detached snippets Sunday by Sunday, with the snippets arranged under subjects, and most likely he has considered them, not in their original context in Scripture, but in isolation, printed in a quarterly. The practice of printing a passage of Scripture in a quarterly or on a lesson leaflet, in order to have it readily available for the pupils and also to facilitate the responsive reading of the lesson in a general session, has been a powerful factor in promoting the disuse of the Bible. Young people can be found who have attended church school regularly and have never once opened a Bible. They have studied fragments of the Bible in quarterlies, but have learned nothing about the use of the Bible as a whole. They are in confusion where to turn to find even the best known passages. It would be a great step forward if all denominations would discontinue the printing of Scripture in quarterlies and insist upon the use of the Bible as a textbook. There needs also to be opportunity on every level, from junior up, for the pupil to become familiar with the structure of the Bible, so that he will know what to look for in its different parts and will have some understanding of how it all fits together. It will be of help to him if he is provided with a story of the Bible that does not merely link together isolated stories but draws out firmly the line of development that runs from one end of the Bible to the other. Individual passages will then be set in a larger context and will cease to be fragments. It is valuable also to have teen-agers read whole books of the Bible on assignment. Some books are quite short and it is usually a surprise to them to find how quickly they can be read. When once they grasp the unity of a whole book and find familiar passages in this larger setting, it is more difficult for them to fall back into their old fragmented impression of Scripture.

Historical framework and background: If the details of the Biblical story are to hang together for anyone and make sense, they need to be built into a solid historical framework. One reason that the Bible falls into fragments for many readers of it is that they have in their minds no such framework. It is like a human body with all the bones removed, which is left a shapeless mass of flesh. Biblical history is not so complicated that it requires an expert to present it in outline. A chart of the main events can be drawn out very simply until it becomes fixed in the minds of the pupils. But what is most important is the application of vivid historical imagination to make the actors in the Biblical story come alive as men and women of flesh and blood. There is an atmosphere of unreality that clings about the Bible in the minds of children and of many adults. In early years most of us have two kinds of stories read to us, Bible stories and fairy stories, and inevitably they become intermingled in our minds, so that Bible land seems to be another species of fairyland. It comes, therefore, as somewhat of a shock to realize that the Biblical characters are real people like ourselves and Palestine a place on this earth where things happen similar to what we see happening round about us. A wide use of maps and of pictures of Palestine can do much to give concreteness; also the reading of travel books about Palestine. George Adam Smith's *Historical Geography of the Holy Land* is still indispensable. It can also be fascinating for young people to learn how archaeologists are digging up the ancient cities of Palestine and casting fresh light upon different periods in its history.

The veil of moralism: The moralistic approach to the Bible, which turns every passage merely into an occasion for moralizing, has put a veil over it that conceals its true meaning and makes it essentially uninteresting. The child is left with the idea that the Bible contains a gallery of saints, good people whom we are to admire and imitate. But in order to make models of character of most Biblical personages, it is necessary to do a little whitewashing, and the zealous moralizers have not shrunk from the task. One fairly recent book on the Old Testament for children completely exonerated Jacob and his mother Rebecca for cheating Esau and lying to Isaac. Jacob was a much better man than Esau and more fitted to be head of the family; therefore, Jacob and Rebecca were merely helping God to get things arranged the way they should be! Stories of David rarely take account of the facts as they are recorded in the books of Samuel. David is idealized, and the barbarous features of his character are explained away or simply ignored. There seem to be no lengths to which some people will not go in order to tidy up the private and public lives of Biblical personages. And so the Bible becomes for the child and youth a book that merely says to him, " Be good."

It is always a relief to young people to discover in their own reading of the Bible that the central characters were not models of perfection, but were mortals like themselves, struggling between good and evil. Abraham, Jacob, David, Jeremiah, Peter, John, Mark and a host of others come alive when we see them in their hours of failure. We begin to grasp that there are no ready-made saints in the Bible. Rather the Bible confronts us with our own humanity in all its heights and depths and opens to us the secret of how it may be redeemed out of the power of darkness and evil into its true fulfillment in the Kingdom of God. The Bible has a dimension of depth that to the moralizer is simply unknown.

The importance of grading: There is good reason to believe that many children have been psychologically conditioned against the Bible by overzealous teachers who have tried to teach them too much of it too soon. These earnest teachers start from the assumption that all of the Bible is good since it is God's Word, and that, if it is good for adults, it should be good also for children. It is the Bible that makes one wise unto salvation. Therefore, a simple but effective way of providing for the child's salvation is to fill him full of texts from the Bible. Whether or not he understands them does not matter too much. They will be like seed in his mind and one day they will sprout and grow. But what actually happens when the child is told a story or made to learn a text which is completely beyond his comprehension is that he is given the impression of a book that he cannot understand even if he tries very hard. The frequent repetition of this experience deepens the impression sharply so that, very early in life, the Bible becomes for him the acme of incomprehensibility.

It is shocking how stupid Christian people can be in this regard. They assume that any story from the Bible should be good for children of any age. Thus, the story of Noah and his ark has been turned into a " delightful " kindergarten tale and its original meaning completely lost. If it were told to small children with the full Biblical content, it would frighten them out of their wits. It is a story strictly for adults, with a profound significance for our Atomic Age which teeters on the brink of self-destruction, but how is one to rescue it from the kindergarten?

The story of Abraham leaving home at God's call may have a rich meaning for teen-agers, but it is lost completely on small children, for whom separation from their family and home is unthinkable. In a church school using uniform lessons in all grades, a kindergarten teacher described Abraham leaving behind his old home and parents and relations, and then, thinking to drive the lesson home, she asked one small boy what he would do if God told him to leave his father and mother, brothers and sisters, and go away to a far country to serve him. She received instantly an honest answer, " I would run and hide behind the big tree."

No one would think of attempting to teach the letter to the Romans to primary children or Ecclesiastes to the kindergarten. But let the material take the form of a story and at once adults are likely to assume that it is useful for the teaching of children. One consequence of this is the false impression that prevails among adults that everything in story form in Scripture is for children and not for adults. They do not expect to find in it an adult meaning. They need to be told that, on the contrary, *nothing* in the Bible was written specifically for children. From beginning to end, it is an adult book. The book of The Proverbs was formulated for the instruction of youth, but for rather mature youths, who were already confronted with the problems of adult life. When we use the Bible with children, as we must do, we should begin by recognizing that we are adapting to the situation of children material that was written for adults, and that the important thing is to retain the original meaning but to interpret it in terms comprehensible to the child. If we water down the meaning or twist the story to give it application in the child's life, we are merely setting up one more obstacle in the way of the child's growth into an understanding of the Bible. Anyone who has tried to write Bible stories for children knows how difficult it is to avoid these pitfalls, and anyone familiar with existing books of Bible stories knows how hard it is to find one in which the author has made an honest effort to retain the meaning of the original stories.

Grading, then, is a necessity in the use of the Bible, but grading does not mean perversion of the Bible in order to get something remotely resembling it that can be used with younger children. Grading simply means that we do not try to make the child take any step in his pilgrimage into the Bible until he is ready for it. It requires an abandonment of the attitude that the child will be benefited by the mere quantity of the Bible with which he is familiar. The purpose of instructing the child in the Scriptures is not just that he may know the Scriptures, but that he may have faith in God as he is revealed in the Scriptures. The quantity of Scripture known is largely irrelevant, for one passage, rightly heard and understood, may open the way to faith, while a hundred passages which have no definite meaning for the child's life may produce only confusion.

There needs to be constant experiment to find what parts of Scripture can be taught most effectively to each age group. Sometimes in the past there has been a tendency to assume that we know with definiteness what children of each age can grasp and absorb and to draw the line very dogmatically. For instance, it was long assumed that primary children could understand nothing of the prophets in the Old Testament. Certainly they could not read the books of the prophets, but in story form they could take in their first impressions of what a prophet was like and so have the foundation laid for a closer acquaintance with prophets at the junior stage. If this is not done, the child inevitably by the age of nine has formed in his mind a false conception of what a prophet is. The Church can learn much from secular education in this matter of grading and should be alert to keep pace in religious training with the mental development of the child in public school.

The variety of literary forms: It would obviate much misunderstanding of Scripture if children, in their study of the Bible, learned to distinguish between the different kinds of writing. They come to it frequently with the assumption that it is all equally a statement of historical facts, and if the suggestion is made that any part is other than that, their minds jump to the conclusion, "Then, it isn't true." This would not happen if their teachers and parents would acquaint them early with the variety of literary forms that are used in the two Testaments: history, legends, hymns, proverbs, parables, sermons, a drama, gospels, letters. God can speak to man through all these different forms of writing. The important thing is to get at the truth that is embodied in any given passage, and failure to recognize the form in which the truth is expressed may result in a failure to hear the truth itself. Thus, for instance, The Book of Jonah, when understood as a parable from the hand of a prophet, embodies a powerful missionary message and reveals a superb literary craftsmanship. But when the attempt is made to read it as history, it becomes a curious story about an utterly absurd prophet, highlighted by the adventures of the prophet in being swallowed by a great fish and vomited forth alive. No one has a right to say that the book *must* be history or *must* be a parable. It is for the record itself to bear witness by its own nature to what it is, and it is for us reverently to recognize its witness to itself and read it as what it claims to be.

The story of creation in the early chapters of Genesis has been a stumbling block to countless people because they have been given to understand that they must read it as history. But even a moment's thought concerning the nature of a historical record is sufficient to enable us to grasp that there could be no historical record of the event of creation, which occurred before any human being was present on the earth. That God is the Creator and that the world and man are his creation is known, not by historical observation, but by faith, and the story of creation is a confession of that faith. It contains knowledge of God and man and the world that are basic to our entire Christian understanding of things. It is real knowledge, knowledge of the truth. But when the record is read, not as a confession of faith but as a detailed history of the first days of the universe, the reader finds himself in a hopeless tangle of contradictions from which he cannot extricate himself, and in which the revelation of the Creator and of the meaning of his creation becomes lost.

The strangeness of the thought forms: The Bible, at many points, even in translation, speaks a different language from that which we ordinarily use today. Translation from Hebrew, Aramaic, and Greek into English should, we assume, bring it within the range of our understanding. But that fails to take account of the differences between our ways of thinking and the ways of thinking that are found in the Bible.

One of the commonest words in the Old Testament, particularly in the books of the prophets, is "judgment"—the judgment of God upon Israel or upon some other nation. It is important also in the New Testament. Behind it lies the conviction that, when a nation sins against God, it brings upon itself some disastrous event which has, at one and the same time, the twin effects of unmasking the sin and of punishing it. God is Lord of history and the nation that disregards his word hears it eventually in the thunderous notes of judgment in history. Both John the Baptist and Jesus proclaimed that a terrifying day of judgment was at hand for Israel, but repentance in the day of judgment could make of it a day of new beginning, the birth of a new creation. Paul's message was that there was no more doom for those who were in Christ Jesus. " Judgment " brought to expression the full force of God's hatred of sin.

Today, the word " judgment " has in general passed out of the religious vocabulary. Men speak of having good judgment and they have a vague idea of a day of judgment at the end of the world, or perhaps upon the death of each person, but they have no thought of a judgment of God that they might be under now. Paul's words about our deliverance from judgment through Christ have no meaning for them. It is as though someone were to go to a group of young people playing ball and were to tell them they no longer had to stay in prison, expecting them to receive the message as good news. But these young people have never been in prison and have no expectation of ever being in prison, so the good news is lost upon them. Modern man, even modern Christian man, does not know what God's judgment is. He is living in a time that is heavy with judgment, when God is writing his judgment upon our civilization in words of fire in the events of our era, but man, having lost the very idea of a judgment, is slow to understand.

We must be willing, therefore, to learn the peculiar language of the Bible. When it uses the word " love," we dare not assume that we know what it means from what we call " love," for the love that is in God and that broke in upon our world in Jesus Christ is different in its nature from the spontaneous passion that men ordinarily call love. When the Bible speaks of " salvation," we dare not equate that with a sudden conversion experience and think we have given the word its full content; rather we must let the Bible itself show us the length and breadth and height and depth of salvation. There is a world of meaning locked up in the Bible that has to be unlocked and explored, and we soon discover that it is not just a world in the Bible but that it is the world of our own true life in God.

A revelation for now: A final criticism of the use of the Bible in church school is that it stops so often at merely giving information about the Bible. A considerable body of information is necessary for an intelligent approach to the Bible and one need not apologize for lessons that confine themselves to giving careful instruction about the background, structure, and history of the Bible. Children need to learn certain facts and to learn them well. But the effort is largely wasted if they stop there. Our purpose in teaching the Bible is that God may speak through it now into the life of the world and into the lives of the children who are being taught by us. Our handling of the Bible must always be with this expectation, that somehow the miracle may happen that God should make his word come alive with the same power in our twentieth century that it had when it was first spoken. For that to happen, we must accept the responsibility of interpreting the ancient word in the modern situation, of hearing the word as it originally sounded in the ears of men and of speaking it in whatever form will bring it home to living persons today. The Bible cannot be left in an ancient setting; it has to be focused upon the actualities of the modern world.

To teach the Scriptures is nothing less than to undertake the ministry of the Word, and that is to put ourselves unconditionally at the service of God that he may speak through us and through our words and actions. To be ministers of the Word is to be taken into the fellowship of the prophets and the apostles, so that we hear what they heard, see what they saw, and have alive in us the same Spirit of God and the some Word of God that were alive in them. For that, we must go far beyond the realm of information. We must be armed with " the sword of the Spirit, which is the word of God." Knowing our Bibles is not sufficient; the decisive question is whether or not we know the God who speaks to us and comes to us as Father, Son, and Holy Spirit in his word in Scripture.

So also, the aim of our teaching must reach far beyond the transmitting of information about the Bible and its contents. We are training children, young people, and adults to be witnessing disciples in a non-Christian world. The power of their witness will be, not their power to quote verses from the Bible, but their power to act and speak in accordance with the faith and life that are manifest in the Bible and that become theirs through the word of the Bible.

The goal of their Bible study, therefore, is that they may know in all his fullness the God who is revealed in the Bible, and may so understand all their life in the light of his presence that not only their words and actions but their very existence will be, moment by moment, a living witness to the reality of God.

may fit in

8

THE GROWTH OF PERSONS

ONE of the most praiseworthy achievements of the religious education movement in the early years of this century, was its focusing of attention upon the person who is to be educated. Its slogan was: " We do not teach subject matter. We teach the child," and its concern was that the whole process of education should be adapted to the observable needs of the child. This constituted a reaction against a type of teaching in which the teacher merely " got up " a lesson on a certain subject and delivered the prepared matter to the class without any very careful consideration as to whether or not the subject matter was relevant to the present experience and needs of the members of the class. As individual persons, each at a different stage in his religious development, they were ignored, and no attempt was made even to discover what their most urgent problems might be. Among kindergarten and primary children it usually meant that the children had poured out upon them a mass of Biblical stories and information, often without any thought being given to the question whether or not the material was within their range of comprehension.

Child study in the secular field had already begun to establish a body of facts concerning the stages in a child's development and to recognize the injury that could be done to a child by forcing upon him decisions and experiences for which he was not yet ready. Also, it was an axiom of educators that all children do not grow at the same rate and each must be permitted to take whatever time he needs to move from one stage to the next. Therefore, before we can rightly teach anyone — child, youth, or adult — we must have some knowledge, not only of human development in general, but of the

specific stages of development at which our pupils now find themselves. Our teaching has as its purpose, not the pouring of a body of
information into their minds, but the lending to them of the assistance that they need now in their growth as Christian persons.

In its zeal to establish this principle, the religious education movement went to unnecessary extremes. There was much talk of a
" child-centered " curriculum in contrast to a " Bible-centered " one,
and the orthodox pattern for curriculum development became, first,
to set down the known needs of the child or youth in order of importance, and then to plan courses through which each of the needs
would be likely to find its satisfaction. It was surprising how little of
the Bible children, youth, and adults seemed to need! And equally
surprising was it to discover that they did not need Christian doctrine at all! The fallacy in the approach was the assumption that it
is a simple matter to discover the needs of persons at various stages
of life. The definition of our needs actually depends upon a number of factors which are not at all obvious. The needs of a youth
who is committed to active Christian discipleship are very different
from the needs of another youth whose chief concern is how he can
have peace of mind and satisfactory relationships with his girl
friends. The needs of a child who is to face life in a situation in which
the Christian faith is constantly contradicted are very different from
the needs of a child for whom it is assumed that a Christian environment will always be present. In short, our reading of the situation of
persons is dependent upon our understanding of the Christian faith,
our conception of what it means to be a Christian, and our estimate
of the world in which they will have to make their way.

A curriculum, religious or secular, based upon the needs of the
child is in danger of becoming a very thin and watery curriculum,
particularly if much weight is allowed to what the child himself
conceives to be his needs. Not many young people of high school age
feel a need to know Latin or French. They have no overpowering
desire to explore the mysteries of Roman civilization or of French
literature. But, if they do not lay the foundations of language study
then, whether they feel the need or not, the doors will be closed
against them later, so that important areas of human experience will
have little meaning for them. It is not always what is at present

most interesting that is permanently most valuable, and a curriculum in our schools that set itself to teach only what was immediately most relevant to the pupil's existing need would be likely to sacrifice many of the most important elements in our cultural heritage. So also a Christian education curriculum that can find little place for the Bible or doctrine or Church history, because they do not meet an observable need of the pupil, may be suspected of forming its estimate of the child in something other than a fully Christian context. It is concerned with what the child needs in order to fulfill an ideal of character which may be only slightly Christian, and not with what the child needs in order one day to grow to his full Christian stature as an intelligent member of a historic Church and an active witnessing disciple of his faith.

Our Understanding of Persons

But who is the child that is delivered into our care? Who is the youth whom we are to educate? Or, to be more specific, where do we find our basic understanding of the human person? Perhaps we have assumed that we know what a human being is. After all, can we not use our eyes and look at the countless specimens of Homo sapiens who pass before our view each day? We have persons close to us in our own homes whom we know intimately. And we have ourselves — not only ourselves now, but our memory of ourselves from our earliest moments of self-consciousness to the present day. How could we fail to know what a human being is? Yet this is a point of great confusion in our time. Man's dilemma, to a very large degree, is that he cannot make up his mind who he is. Sometimes he thinks that he is nothing more than an animal with a highly developed brain. Sometimes he goes to the opposite extreme and thinks that he is divine. Often he fluctuates between variant conceptions of himself and lives in a state of inner bewilderment and dividedness.

Man's estimate of himself depends upon his faith concerning himself. Only a part of his being is subject to observation, even by himself or by the most skillful devices of the psychologists. The roots of his nature reach far into the unseen and nothing is truer than the statement that man is a mystery. His nature is a mystery, even as the nature of God is a mystery. He cannot know who he is with the simple clarity with which he knows that two and two make four. He has to commit himself to one or other of a limited number of possible beliefs concerning himself. And what he believes concerning himself and other human beings will have a profound influence, not only upon his understanding of his own experiences, but upon all his relationships in life.

A Christian doctrine of man is thus basic to any program of Christian education. A program that operates with something less than or other than a Christian understanding of persons is likely to produce something less than or other than Christian persons. The starting point for a Christian in his definition of true humanity is Jesus Christ. He is, for us, not only the revelation of the nature of God but also the revelation of the nature of man. To be human in our relationships with other people is to be mastered, as Jesus was, by a love that overcomes self and penetrates the misery of the other man. To be inhuman is to be mastered by self and so insulated from our neighbor that any real understanding of his experience is impossible. The humanity of Jesus is a humanity that is what it is because of God. He is the fulfillment of humanity in the sense of being the completion of humanity, but only because in each moment he is filled with the Holy Spirit and lives out of the infinite resources of God. To be human is to be made in the likeness of God, merciful as he is merciful, just as he is just, true as he is true, holy as he is holy, and it is the perfection of that likeness to God in Jesus that is the perfection of his humanity.

It begins to be clear, then, that man cannot be defined in isolation, as though he had a self-sufficient existence within the borders of his own being. He is bound together both with God and with his fellow man in such a way that his nature can be described only when all three have their rightful place in the picture. He does not exist alone. To be alone, that is, cut off from God and from his fellow man, is to be deprived of his existence. What man is in his relationships, vertically with God and horizontally with his fellow men, is what he is, and each relationship is dependent on the other. They are really not two but one.

The new man in Christ, of whom Paul speaks, is not a peculiar religious kind of man, but simply man as God intends him to be. He is called a new man because he has put behind him his old self-centered being, however cultured and virtuous it may be, and has begun life afresh with God as the sovereign center of his being. He is born of the Holy Spirit, or has received the Holy Spirit, which simply means that God, who has come into our humanity in Jesus Christ, comes now actually into *my* humanity, so that he dwells in me as in a temple and by his word and Spirit determines all things in my existence. But — let us make no mistake — this is not a special Christian variety of humanity; it is the manifestation of what it means to be, in the fullest sense, a human being. This is what man was created to be when God made him in his likeness. The loss of this nature by man was the loss of his humanity. And Christ's work of redemption was a work of restoration, restoring to man the nature that God intended should be his from the beginning.

But this is not man as we meet him in ourselves and in our fellow men. The man whom we know best is not man in the likeness of God, but man in the most radical unlikeness to God — not a God-determined, God-centered man, but a stubbornly self-centered man. If God made man in his own likeness, then something has happened to frustrate the design of God and to pervert man's nature. The answer of the Scriptures and of the Christian faith is that man sinned against God; lured by the prospect of being his own god, he defied the will of God and brought himself under the dark shadow of guilt. It is symbolic that, in Genesis, Adam's cutting himself apart from God is followed by Cain's wanton slaying of his brother Abel. Sin, by divorcing a man from God, leaves him in darkness, and his enmity toward God is transmuted into a blind and unreasoning hatred of his fellow man. In isolation from God he quickly loses his humanity. Sin, therefore, has to be defined in two dimensions: it is a proud self-centeredness which both alienates a man from God and disrupts his relationships with his fellow men. But no matter how deeply a man becomes entangled in sin, he does not cease to be a man who was made in the likeness and image of God. The image of God may be totally defaced in him on the surface of his life, but deep beneath the surface the remembrance remains of what his humanity was intended to be. He cannot get free from the haunting sense of a destiny that, if it were fulfilled, would give a different meaning to his existence. When he sees inhumanity in all its naked horror, he shrinks back from it as a contradiction of his nature. Yet he loves to be master of himself and tries to work out schemes of life that will leave him his self-mastery while yet avoiding the disorders that arise from his self-centeredness Eventually, however, he is without power to control the forces within his own self or to limit their destructiveness.

The doctrine of original sin has sometimes been interpreted as an assertion that man, in his original nature, was sinful. It means rather that we are born into a humanity whose alienation from God influences our development long before we are ever conscious of it. There is in us a propensity toward self-centeredness. The drift of life is such that we have only to refrain from making any decisions to be carried ever more deeply into sin. We are a part of sinful humanity, the depth of whose involvement in sin is revealed in the cross. It is in the heart of humanity, even the most virtuous and religious humanity, to crucify the Son of God, and not by accident, but because, as the revealer of the will of God, he is an affront to the proud will of man.

Man, therefore, when he awakens to self-consciousness, is confronted with a contradiction within himself. He finds himself torn between a nature which has much support from the world around him and of which the ruling principle is self-assertion and self-advantage, and a nature that goes in a totally opposite direction. He does not of himself recognize the former as a sinful nature. Rather, it is only as he comes to know God and to find his human destiny in the will of God that he has eyes to see the significance of those forces in life that rob him of his destiny. The man who has no knowledge of God can have no knowledge of sin. Our understanding of the disorder of our life as sin is a direct consequence of knowing ourselves as God knows us, seeing ourselves in his light. If God did not reveal himself to us in his Word, and in revealing himself reveal us to ourselves, we should not know sin. We should know contradiction, disharmony, confusion, inner conflict and anxiety, but we should not know sin. It is wrong, therefore, to think that either children or adults can know that they are sinners by being told that they are or by having their sins pointed out to them. It is the knowledge of God in his love and mercy toward them, and in his truth and justice, that alone can make them know that they are sinners.

A Christian doctrine of man, then, has always to say two things, which at first seem contradictory. It says that man's only true nature is the likeness of God as we see it in the nature of Jesus Christ. At once our natural reaction is to protest that what the Christian faith expects of us is "beyond human nature." But when we hear the second word of the gospel concerning man, that he is a sinner, imprisoned within himself by the power of sin dwelling in him, and unable merely by the use of his own resources to attain his true life, we accuse the Christian gospel of taking an unreasonably dark view of man, of making him much blacker and weaker than he really is. But when we do this, we are falling into the absurdity of accusing the gospel of being both too optimistic and too pessimistic concerning man. Sometimes the plea is heard, from some quarters within the Church, for a scaling down both of what is expected of man and of the emphasis upon sin. Christian truth, however, calls, not for a softening, but for a sharpening of the edges of the contradiction, for it is the contradiction between man in Christ and the natural man in his own self-centeredness. That he is unable to save himself does not mean that he is unable to attain a respectable measure of morality and religiousness. The moral and spiritual superiority of the Pharisees who rejected Jesus is surely proof of that. But he is unable, by his own efforts, to deliver himself from the thralldom of his own self-centeredness and to find the truly God-centered life for which he is destined. To be born of God cannot be man's achievement, but must be received by him as God's work in him and God's gift to him of his own life.

FALSE VIEWS OF MAN IN CHRISTIAN EDUCATION

It should not be difficult to recognize the importance of the doctrine of man for our entire approach to Christian education. An inadequate doctrine of man means an inadequate understanding both of ourselves and of those whom we teach. To teach effectively we must know our pupils from the inside. Our personal impressions and observations are important but not sufficient. We need to know them in the depths of their being, and, as we have already shown, that is a knowledge of human beings that comes to us only as God, through the word of the Scriptures, sets their lives in the light of his truth. We shall know who our pupils are only as we know who we ourselves are, by letting our entire existence come under the light of God's presence.

Moralism of every kind rests upon a superficial reading of the nature of the human person. The assumption is that conduct is to be molded by the mind and the will without too much difficulty, and that what the pupil needs is to be shown plainly the difference between right and wrong. Inspire him with noble ideals of what life should be, and, although he may not realize them completely, his life will be transformed by his incessant endeavor to reach them. To suggest to him that he has not in himself the power to reach the Christian ideal is to cut the nerve of his effort. One has only thus to describe the moralistic approach to recognize how widely prevalent it is.

Moralism has in it a sub-Christian view of man. It fails to take account of how deep the roots of conduct are, and that disorder in conduct usually has beneath it, not just an ignorance of what is right, but a disorder in the self that renders it incapable of right action. The Christian doctrine of man's imprisonment in sin alone takes account of this depth of the problem. Secondly, a passionate adherence to noble ideals may lead to self-deception, the person either modifying the Christian ideal to bring it within his grasp or concealing from himself how contrary his actual life is to the ideals to which he is committed. Both can cause serious inner conflicts. The Christian doctrine does not remove the conflict, but changes it from an unfruitful to a fruitful one, from being intolerable to being inevitable. The natural man, in his proud self-centeredness, it says, is incapable of living the life of the Kingdom. To be poor in spirit, meek, merciful as God is merciful, and pure in heart, is beyond his competence. There has to be a conquest of the self by the Spirit of God so that his life begins to be lived from a new center, where his inmost self bows in unconditional surrender under the sovereignty of God. In short, only where the sovereignty of God is established in this intimate personal way is the life of God's Kingdom possible.

Equally inadequate is the understanding of the human person in certain evangelistic approaches which have been, at times, widely operative in the church school. The assumption here is that the child is a sinner by nature from birth and, as such, is completely unable to understand anything of Christian truth. Blindness is total. The only way in which this blindness of sin can be broken through is by conversion. Therefore, it is futile to try to teach the child. The only reasonable procedure is to use every possible opportunity to convict him of sin and to lead him to repentance and regeneration. The age of the child is of no importance. A four-year-old sinner, a fourteen-year-old sinner, and a twenty-four-year-old sinner are all in equal peril and their only hope is conversion. The church school program divides thus into two parts: the conversion of the sinners, and the instruction of the converted that they may grow in grace.

There are two main errors in this approach. One is the denial of what is affirmed in Scriptures, that man, in spite of his sin, remains the child of God. The prodigal, returning from the far country, heard from his father not the words, " You are a sinner," but the gracious words, " You are my son." Therefore, no matter how deeply a man has fallen into sin, our point of contact with him is our knowledge that beneath it all he is a child of God, and that, however broken his relationship with God may be, he cannot break God's relationship with him. He cannot deliver himself out of the hand of God. He cannot cease to be God's creation. Our entire approach to him must express, not primarily condemnation of his sin, but recognition of him as the child of God that he is. And if this is true of the hardened adult sinner, how much more must it be true of the child and of the youth! We have no delusions about the reality of sin in them, and the obstacle that sin is likely to be between them and God, and we may have to speak to them pointedly concerning it. But our starting point with them is the fact that they belong to God, that God is their Father, and that he is at work in their lives long before they can consciously understand anything of his purposes. It is God's pleasure to be, not only the God of the parent, but also the God of the child from earliest years. He has set us in families that the child, from his first moments, may share the life of the parent, not only physically but spiritually, and that in the intimacy of the home the child may never know a time when he does not look trustfully to God as his Father and to Jesus as the center and source of all life. A doctrinaire denial that there can be any true faith or any knowledge of God until conversion has taken place, does violence to Christian truth at many points. It actually rests upon the assumption that until conversion man is by nature a sinner, in complete isolation from God, rather than a child of God, belonging to God, but with the order of his life distorted and perverted by sin.

The second error is in the sharp division that is made between the state of sin and the state of grace, and the idea that only by a sudden conversion does anyone pass from the one to the other. Sin is the resistence of our human wills to God's will and it remains as a factor to be reckoned with as long as we live. We never reach a stage in our development when we no longer have in honesty to bow before God and cry, " Lord, be merciful to me a sinner." Therefore, the converted cannot take their stand above the sinner, pointing down at him with accusing finger, but have to take their place humbly alongside him, united with him in need of the mercy of God. The Christian, no matter how soundly converted he may be, is on the way to becoming a self-righteous Pharisee if he has ceased to feel his solidarity with his fellow man in sin. Nor should those who experience a sudden conversion require of all others an experience similar to their own. God calls men and binds them to himself in many different ways. The idea that only by a sudden emotional crisis can the ultimate decision of faith be reached leaves many people waiting for something to happen to them, when God has already been calling them in quiet ways and they have been hungering and thirsting for him without knowing that their hunger and thirst were evidences of God's Spirit at work in them.

GROWTH VS. CONVERSION

We turn now from one extreme to the other. In reaction to the moralistic and the evangelistic approach in the church school, there has grown up a type of education that has in it no place for any mention of sin, repentance, or conversion. The child is to grow like a flower, stage by stage, until his character blossoms forth into its full Christian form. The purpose of Christian education is to surround the child with influences that will promote this growth. There should never be a time when he has the slightest doubt that he is a Christian. He must learn to recognize his faults and failings, but to call them sins is likely to burden him with a sense of guilt that will only impede his progress. In a process of growth there are bound to be imperfect stages and mistakes, but they can be forgotten as one passes on to greater heights.

In a church school where most of the children have grown up in Christian homes, in which belief in God, respect for Jesus, and a fairly high standard of morality are part of the environment, this approach has a strong appeal. It seems an unwarrantable slur upon such children to suggest that they have ever been anything except Christians. Religiously and morally they are superior to most other children in the community, and they themselves would have difficulty in understanding why any radical repentance or conversion should be needed in their lives; improvement certainly, growth in knowledge and virtue, but not the death of an old self and the birth of a new one. Sin and guilt, repentance and conversion, are appropriate to people who are irreligious and immoral, whose lives are a defiance of God, but not to the solid, respectable Christian folk of the community or their offspring!

This optimism about the person who has a Christian background is, by some, extended to man in general, and we begin then to hear that man is by nature good. He requires, not redemption, but only enlightenment. He does not intend evil, but falls into it as a consequence of inadequate education and perverted institutions. Give him the education he deserves and purify the economic and political structure of society, if you wish to establish the Kingdom of God on earth. Understandably, this point of view leads to a passionate concern with education, for education is to deliver mankind from all its disorder and unhappiness; also to a passion for the transformation of the economic and political order. But in a time such as the present, when the reality of evil as a force working from within men compels the attention of the world, such romantic conceptions of human nature have a hollow ring. They are totally unable to take account of the phenomena with which we are confronted in our fellow men and in ourselves. Also, we begin to be aware that the good Christian, who has little that he can call sin and no conscious need for repentance, has actually substituted a very smug middle-class form of religion and morality for New Testament Christianity and may be considered, perhaps, the most stubborn obstacle to the rebirth of an evangelizing Church. He and his children have been inoculated against a real Christian faith by the polite form of it to which they have become accustomed. Moral and religious growth may therefore be nothing more than the elaboration of lines of development which lead, not to any new triumph of Christ in his Church or in the world, but rather to the consolidation of Pharisaism in the Church and the increase of complacency in man in general.

Conversion, then, must still have a place in Christian education. The word must be liberated from the narrow connotation it so often has and must be used, as it is in Scripture, to describe the transformation which takes place in our human life with each fresh in-breaking of God upon us. When God comes to us in his Word and Spirit, a question mark is set against our whole existence, we recognize our unlikeness to God as sin, and, repenting of it, are changed by his power into a nearer likeness to him. Therefore, all teaching of the gospel, by its very nature, has in it the possibility, and should have the expectation, of producing a transformation of life. The word of God, because it is the word *of God,* is always a converting word, not just in the first hearing of it, but in every hearing of it. Thus, when Jesus says that man shall live, not by bread alone, but by every word that proceeds out of the mouth of God, he is saying that man, all of his life long, must have his heart open to that word of God which judges him, brings him to repentance and so to new life in God.

Conversion, therefore, is not to be set in antithesis to moral and spiritual growth. In the parable of the Growing Grain, Jesus sets before us the nature of Christian growth. For growth to take place at all, there must first be a sowing of the seed of truth. The preacher and the teacher are sowers. But the growth is not in their hands. For a time no result of the sowing is visible. Then a tiny shoot breaks through the ground. The stalk becomes strong and produces an ear, but only an empty one. Then finally the ear fills and the precious grain is ripened. God takes his own time in the growing of a man. The whole work may be spoiled if the sower becomes impatient at the various incomplete stages. To expect of an eight-year-old child a result that is not due until he is eleven, is to do violence both to the child and to the work of God. It is a marvelous conversion that takes place between the planting of the seed and the ripening of the grain, but the sower is directly warned that it is not in his power to bring it about. His work is to sow the seed faithfully and to wait for the growth. There is a work of harvesting also, and the sower dare not forget that he is also a harvester. There comes a decisive point in the life of every Christian, or there may be several points, at which he is ready to move out into a greatly increased fruitfulness in his faith. At such points he needs help to make the transition. It is with him as with those people who were Socrates' care, whose minds were ready for independent thought but who needed a midwife to bring them to the birth. But here it is not just the mind, but the entire being, the soul of the Christian, that is to be reborn. The teacher, as well as the preacher, must understand the importance of these harvest times and be ready to give the help that persons need in passing from one stage of Christian development to the next.

THE LIMITATIONS OF TEACHING

The parable of the Growing Grain is also a reminder to the educator of what he cannot do. Sometimes one comes upon statements of educators that seem to assume that they can control the development of human character. Education becomes a technique for manipulating character. The grossest forms of this are in totalitarian countries, where education is an arm of the Government for producing the kind of citizens that the National Plan requires. The citizen is designed as a piece of machinery is designed, and then the educator goes to work on the production of a curriculum that can be counted on to produce such persons en masse. But it is not only in totalitarian countries that this idea finds entrance. The advances of recent years in psychological knowledge and in educational techniques make it very easy for educators in democratic countries to fall into the habit of thinking in terms of " controlling the responses of human beings for desirable ends." It is so important, in a day when our civilization is shaken, to multiply the number of persons who can be depended upon to think the right things, say the right things, and fight for the right things! So education loses those elements which make for the birth of courageous, independent minds and becomes the means of conditioning the nation's future citizens that they may all be as close as possible to the desired pattern.

A Church program of education is always in danger of falling into this same groove, and the Christian educator is in danger of thinking that he has in his hands a technique for producing Christians of a certain type. Education that proceeds upon such an assumption is nothing less than blasphemous. It has in it a fundamental disrespect both for God and for man.

The fact that God chose to come to man in a word has in it an infinite respect for the freedom and integrity of the human person. God is not willing to compel faith or obedience in any man. They have no value for him unless they are the free expression of a man's own being. Each man has to see for himself, to believe with his own soul, to know with his own mind, to choose by the free action of his own will, so that his faith and obedience are entirely his own. The Church has, far too often in the past, disowned this principle, being more anxious that men should conform to Christian standards of faith and conduct than that they should find their way to an immediate personal knowledge of God in his Word and Spirit. What we should be looking for is not agreement with what we say, but aliveness to the truth and to the problems in life with which the truth confronts us. This aliveness may express itself in doubt or even antagonism at first, while indifference is yielding an instant agreement. We do not want to control the responses of those whom we teach, because control of that kind, even for the noblest ends, means dealing with them as something other than the children of God that they are. Rather, we are anxious to lead them to the point where they discover their own true self-control in coming unconditionally under the control of God's Spirit. It may seem contradictory, yet it is profoundly true, that only in subjection to God do they find perfect freedom.

THE LARGER DIMENSIONS OF EDUCATION

The teacher in the church school must never forget that what happens there can be at best only a fragment of the total religious education of the child or youth. That education begins with the child's first experience of the meaning of life. Countless factors enter into it: persons, events, the atmosphere of the home, the neighborhood group, school studies and experiences, inner ponderings, books, radio and television programs, picture shows. The sight of a dead bird may set a child to puzzling over the meaning of death. A sentence overheard in passing on the street may lodge in the mind and set up a ferment. A decisive moment in religious development for a youth may arrive as he rides on the streetcar, or paddles a canoe across the lake in summer, or lies in bed at night, or talks with a friend about something that would hardly be considered religious. It would be nonsense for us to think that we can control the spiritual growth of our pupils. Their spiritual growth is a secret, unpredictable matter which cannot be channeled into the official hours of church school or church.

Our part as Christian teachers is to open to them the resources of Christian truth that they may understand what God is doing with them in the whole of their experience. It is God who educates them, and for their education he uses every event of their lives, both great and small. Nothing is without its meaning for their development. A crushing misfortune may do more to give them understanding of the deeper levels of human experience than years of sermons and study. Or it may have an embittering, blinding effect. Which effect it has depends, however, upon the person's understanding of the world and of his relationship to the Power behind the world and its events. Therefore, the vital function of the church and church school is not to explain all human experience, but to bring together, in a living way, the person who is confronted with the mystery of the meaning of the world and the Christian revelation of God which alone is the key to the mystery.

It is God who educates. We may serve him in an essential way, an indispensable way, as servants of his word of revelation. But God is upon the scene before we arrive and he has been at work in the life of the child long before we begin our teaching. We do not make a person a child of God by telling him that God is his Father. He has been a child of God from the beginning and our words do no more than make him aware who he is. The truth which the gospel proclaims to a man corresponds to the reality of his life, but he has not eyes to see what is directly before him and all about him until the gospel takes away his blindness. Education, then, is a process far vaster than anything we can organize; it goes on constantly; it can no more be stopped than we can stop the turning of the world. It goes on for a lifetime. There are no intermissions. There never arrives a day midway in life when God says, "I have finished the education of this man." But if the book of revelation and redemption is closed, God's work of education in a man's life remains for him a jumble of incomprehensible experiences. It does not make sense. The Bible is essential to the fruitfulness of education, because in it alone does a man discover what God has been doing with him through the years, and why.

We can understand the importance, then, of a close co-ordination between the courses studied in the church school and the present life experience of the pupil. The purpose of the study is to provide the light in which the situations of life take on their true Christian meaning and the pupil finds, in the Christian faith, the key to the mystery of life.

9

THE CHRISTIAN HOME

THE three major agencies of Christian education are the church school, the church in its worship and fellowship, and the home. We have seen in Chapter 3 that in Old and New Testament times the parent in the home carried the primary responsibility for the education of his children in the faith, and that the father was recognized as having a priestly function. Again in the Reformation the home came into prominence and both parents were expected to guide the children and young people in the study of the Bible and the catechisms and to lead them regularly in worship.

Robert Burns has left for us in " The Cotter's Saturday Night " a picture of a rural home in Scotland that had its character stamped upon it by its faith. The members of the family gathered round the table after the evening meal, the father with the big family Bible before him,

> " And ' Let us worship God! ' he says, with solemn air.
> They chant their artless notes in simple guise;
> They tune their hearts, by far the noblest aim:
> Perhaps ' Dundee's ' wild warbling measures rise,
> Or plaintive ' Martyrs,' worthy of the name.
>
> . . . .
>
> The priest-like father reads the sacred page,
> How Abram was the friend of God on high;
>
> . . . .
>
> Or Job's pathetic plaint, and wailing cry;
> Or rapt Isaiah's wild, seraphic fire;
>
> . . . .

> Then kneeling down, to Heaven's Eternal King,
> The saint, the father, and the husband prays:
> Hope 'springs exulting on triumphant wing,'
> That thus they all shall meet in future days.
>
> .   .   .   .
>
> From scenes like these old Scotia's grandeur springs,
> That makes her loved at home, revered abroad."

Family religion two hundred years ago was not always so beautiful and impressive as this. It could be a fearful thing for sensitive and intelligent children when earnest but ignorant parents pressed upon them incessantly what they considered to be the saving truths of the Christian faith. David Hume suffered intensely in his home under the ministrations of his parents and relatives, and his skepticism was no doubt accentuated by his early experiences of a narrow and unintelligent faith. Edmund Gosse, in *Father and Son,* has left us a graphic record of his struggle for freedom against the determination of a narrowly evangelical father to make the son conform to his own religious views, and it should serve as a warning for all time of the harm that can be done by a well-meaning Christian parent.

There is little likelihood today, however, of many children being injured by having religion forced upon them in the home. The pendulum has swung to the opposite extreme, and, even among the most earnest Christian people, little is done beyond the years of early childhood to teach children in the home anything concerning the Christian faith. Family worship has, in general, vanished. The father has bowed out of action almost entirely, and the mother, if she reads Bible stories and teaches little prayers to her children in the years before they start to school, feels that she has discharged her duty and can hand over the remainder of the task to the church school teacher. A group of teachers from eighteen churches in a metropolitan area, when asked what percentage of children in their classes received no Christian instruction at home, ranged from 90 to 98 per cent in their estimates. None considered that more than one child in ten was taught at home. Even parents who hold high office in the Church and show their Christian concern by their activities in the community are found often never to have engaged in discussions with their children concerning any aspects of the Christian faith. The development has reached such an extreme that we can speak of an abdication by the Christian parent of his function as a minister of the faith to his own children. This abdication is one of the salient factors in the present situation, and both its causes and its consequences will bear investigation.

The Decline of the Home as a Christian Force

No subject calls forth such floods of sentimental rhetoric and declamation as the Christian home. Oh, the good old days when every Christian family met around the family altar and children had a holy reverence for their parents, when the atmosphere of the home was almost like the atmosphere of a church! Those were the days, and all that we have to do to get back to them is to reinstitute family worship in the home! The problem is rather more complex than that, and we must dispense both with nostalgia about the past and with embarrassment about our present failings if we are to make progress in our consideration of it. When we reconstruct the past upon the basis of valid historical records, it turns out to be much less ideal than it appears through the mists of mingled memory and legend. Every age has its own peculiar advantages and its own peculiar forms of unfaithfulness, and there is no reason to consider our own worse than those of a century or two centuries ago. But we do need to understand our own situation and our own problem.

First, we must recognize that the structure of the home has changed radically in the past century. The family that Robert Burns describes was a close-knit unit, combining within itself a large number of functions. The sons worked with the father upon the land, producing food for the entire family and some for sale in the nearest market to gain a little ready cash. The mother and some of the daughters processed the food, spun the wool that came from the sheep and wove it into cloth for garments, and, if necessary, helped with some of the outside work. If sons or daughters could be spared from home, they went to work with neighboring farmers, but the home remained their center of interest, entertainment, and devotion.

Recreation was simple, and was provided in their own home or in that of their friends nearby. From daylight to dark, from week end to week end, the whole of life's activities circled round the home, and, apart from the weekly worship in the church, religion also was a function of the family.

Except in isolated regions, the home no longer in the modern world retains that structure. It is unrealistic sentimentalism to talk of its restoration. It is also dishonest, because neither men nor women have any intention of returning to that primitive order. We have moved from a predominantly agrarian to a predominantly industrial economy, with the consequence that a large part of the population lives in towns and cities. Also, in the country modern inventions have changed the entire way of life to make it conform to the pattern of the city.

The functions of the family have been stripped from it one by one like layers from an onion. The men of the family scatter to their work in various places and are gone all day. The sons most likely find their opportunities in other communities, so that they no longer live at home. Food and clothing are purchased in the stores instead of being processed or manufactured at home, and the daughters (and perhaps also the mother) are free to take work outside the home. The children may attend school close to home at first so that they are at home for lunch, but soon their higher education takes them farther away, and they, like the others, are gone all day. From breakfast in the morning until dinner at night, only the mother remains in the home, and most likely she too will be somewhere else for part of the day. In many instances dinner in the evening will be the first occasion on which all members of the family have seen each other that day, and the first chance they have had to discuss together anything that has happened in the past twenty-four hours. But after dinner the family scatter again, the younger members to their homework and bed, the older members to their several engagements. Recreation is mainly outside the home. The motor car makes it easy to get away. Television is supposed to be reversing this trend and keeping families at home, but if they sit all evening in darkness and in silence, they may not actually be with each other at all. They may be as separated as though they were sitting in the local movie house. This situation may be so accentuated in some instances that the home is little more than a hotel where the members of the family sleep and eat. Even where they make a determined effort to have time for shared activities, there is a constant awareness of the slim margin of time they have for their common life. It is within this structure that the Christian family has to reclaim its heritage. Many of the changes in the home that are lightly attributed to the modern degeneracy of Christians are actually the result of this drastic revolution in the order of the family.

We must also make allowance for a reaction against all forms of piousness that has affected wide areas of modern society. The evangelical revival, when it had spent its original force, thinned out in many places into a type of religiousness that made up in verbosity for what it lacked in depth. Stock phrases tended to flow far too easily. A pious tone of voice, a pious look, and an ability to use pious language were taken as the marks of a converted man. But to solid, thoughtful people this piosity was utterly distasteful. They could not endure it. And yet they were constantly having it suggested to them that the absence of these marks from their own conversation and demeanor was an indication that they were not saved. The only people they knew who talked about religion talked in these terms. Religious speech was fixed in their minds as pious speech. But pious speech was a totally inadequate form of expression for their own deeper thoughts about life and God. Better by far to be silent than to talk like that! And their silence on questions of faith with family and friends was an expression of their reverence before the mysteries of life and of faith. It would have been liberation for them to have found a new form of Christian language in which they could have spoken naturally and without undue emotion about these things. But the language was not there for them and it was not in their power to create it.

Closely combined with this was the tendency of modern man to rely on moral influence, rather than upon explicit teaching, upon character rather than upon truth: " It is not what you say that counts but what you are." A favorite motto was, " What you are speaks so loudly that I cannot hear what you say." As a protest against words and doctrine that had not the integrity of a life behind them, there was a certain validity in this. But too easily it passed over into a moralistic self-confidence, like that of a woman who hotly denied that a parent was remiss who was silent about the Christian faith with her children. "I do not need to say anything about religion to my children," she asserted; "my example is sufficient." Phillips Brook's phrase, "Truth mediated through personality," was misinterpreted to mean that truth does not need to be mediated in any other way than through personality, that the expression of the truth in comprehensible words is quite unnecessary. The smug complacency of a parent who tells himself that his personality has so much of truth in it that nothing more is needed to complete his Christian ministry to his children is not hard to detect, and when this is used as a basis for evading the responsibility of coherent Christian conversation in the home, it becomes a serious matter.

Yet another factor influencing parents has been the warning they have heard against unfair indoctrination of their children. They have had psychologists point out to them the harm that can be done to growing personalities if parents use their authority to make their children think exactly as they do themselves. The child can be robbed of his opportunity to think for himself and can become merely a shadow of the parent, with no strength or stability or initiative of his own. Such a child lives in a state of mental and emotional slavery and may be warped for life by it. The impression, therefore, has gone abroad that the intelligent thing to do is to let children and young people work things out for themselves, without interference of any kind. Far better to say nothing to them about the Christian faith than to run the risk of exerting an unfair or unhealthy influence upon them. Most intelligent of all, then, would be the parent who maintains complete impartiality on the subject of religion and is indifferent which of the religions of the world his offspring may choose to follow. Let them make up their minds for themselves which has in it the most truth, when they are old enough to examine the evidence. Impartiality of this kind makes a strong appeal to a scientific age.

But why should this impartiality be applied only in respect to religion? Even the most intelligent parent is unlikely to feel any need to conceal from his children his convictions concerning international affairs, concerning policies to be followed in the community or in the state, concerning the right use of money and time, and concerning a wide variety of personal habits. The newborn babe is not consulted whether or not he wants to live in the house which his parents at present occupy, and, if he shows a distaste for it at five, they are not likely to feel that they are imposing upon him if they refuse to move. Nor is the small boy expected to make a decision for himself whether or not he will wash himself when he gets up in the morning. A child does not and cannot start from scratch in life, for he enters a complex world and a complex culture which will inevitably exert a profound influence upon the shaping of his life before he is prepared to make any decisions of his own. The wise parent will let him begin making decisions of his own at the earliest possible moment, but he will also see to it that he is as well-informed as possible in each matter on which he makes a decision. He will not withhold from him information that is essential to the right understanding of any problem merely through fear of influencing him unduly, but will instruct him, at the same time taking care not to make the decision for him.

All teaching involves a danger of some measure of coercive indoctrination, but we do not for that reason abandon our schools and colleges that our children may be free to discover the truth for themselves. Rather, we continue the teaching and encourage in the child or youth the courage to think for himself and to trust what he sees for himself in preference to all that is told him, even though it be upon the most impressive authority. As parents, we make plain to them that we are not infallible, and that it is their duty to contradict us if what we say seems to them to be untrue. Our responsibility is to tell them as honestly as we can what we have learned of the truth, but to warn them that our best knowledge is not sufficient for them — that they must, with their own eyes and with their own minds and with their own hearts, come to a knowledge of the truth for themselves.

There are undoubtedly other influences that have contributed to the decline of Christian teaching in the home. The sheer busyness of parent and child alike has something to do with it. There are so many interests and activities to occupy the mind that it is easy for religion to get crowded out. The tempo of modern life, unchecked, is rather too fast for contemplation or for conversation about the great deep central questions of existence. There is also the fact that in most of the novels published for several generations, religion is ignored in the picture of life that is drawn. That is changing at the present time, and the naturalness with which characters in novels engage in religious discussion may well have an effect upon those who read the novels.

We must admit too that, in the general pattern of the modern church, there had ceased to be any expectation that the parent would do much in the way of Christian teaching. After the first few years of the child's life the church school took over that task and the parent was free of it. The parent might be urged to help Johnny with his Sunday School lesson, but he was provided with no materials to equip him for anything more. The church school curriculum was planned essentially for a teacher and pupils, not for teacher, parents, and pupils. The parent was on the outside, looking in. It was not illogical for him to form the conviction that he had no very important place in the Church's program of education. All these forces together have combined to bring about the abdication by the Christian parent of his teaching function and the emptying of the home of much of its Christian significance.

If we have done no more than make clear the complexity of the problem, it will be worth-while. Many parents are aware that their children need religious training and that they themselves have primary responsibility for it, but at this point they meet their worst frustration, for they seem unable to speak, or, if they do speak, their children seem unable to hear. No facile explanations of this are of any value. Above all, pious exhortation or angry scoldings of parents is out of place, for it presupposes that the only obstacle is the indifference of the parent. It may help the parent to know that he is entangled in a problem that reaches far beyond himself, involving the whole Church and the character of Christianity in our time. And if once he sees how he came into this predicament and what are the consequences of his abdication, he may have a more urgent desire to find the way out.

THE MINISTRY OF THE PARENT

Horace Bushnell, one hundred years ago, brought forcefully to recognition the mutual involvement of parent and child with each other. The parent cannot by any means escape exerting a decisive influence upon the development of the child. Just as the unborn baby lives within the body of the mother, drawing its very lifeblood from her, so the small child lives within the body of the family, determined in his entire existence by the atmosphere, ideas, standards, and faith that permeate the life of the family and give to it its character. He may very early begin to rebel against certain elements in the family life, so that the influence becomes one of repulsion rather than attraction; nevertheless, the inescapable starting point of all his thinking and living will be whatever has met him and become a part of him in those early years of almost complete dependence. The more intimate the life of the home and the more completely the parents command the respect and love of the child, the more powerful will be the direct influence.

It is a delusion to think that a parent who says nothing about religion to his child has no religious influence upon the child. There is a remarkable transparency to life within the home that makes it practically impossible for any member of the family to conceal what he really believes. The underlying convictions and principles express themselves in action and word so that, day by day, a picture is built up of what lies beneath the surface. It is impossible for a child not to notice what his parents value most in life. If their one consuming passion is business or social success, he knows it. If God comes first with them and they would be willing to lose a business deal or miss out on a social engagement rather than compromise their principles, he knows it. In short, the religion of the parent, whatever it is, is more powerful than any other influence in determining what is to be the religious direction of the child's life.

Often, the parent unconsciously negates the effect of the teaching being given in the church school. A junior child is studying the meaning of Christian fellowship and the teacher deals particularly with the need for Christians to show kindness to strangers. But the parents of one child in the class are fixed in a social pattern in which they mingle with four or five other congenial couples and ignore everyone else in the community and in the church. If strangers sit in the same seat with them during worship, they do not even see them. What likelihood is there of the teaching of the church school breaking through the narrow pattern which the parents' example fastens upon the child? It is possible, but not easy to accomplish. How different it would be if the parents were equally concerned that the child should grow up with a Christian attitude toward strangers! The parent cannot escape responsibility for the religious shaping of his child's life.

The solidarity of the family in its faith comes to expression at various points in Scripture. In the Old Testament, the decision of the father as the head of the house was a decision, not for himself alone, but for his entire household. The call of Abraham inevitably involved his wife and servants and later his son. Joshua quite naturally says, " As for me and my house, we will serve the Lord " (Josh. 24:15), assuming that his decision determines not only his personal stand but also that of all who are allied with him within the household of which he is head. Thus, in the New Testament, we find in the book of The Acts the practice of baptizing households. The Roman centurion Cornelius had with him his kinsmen and near friends when he heard the gospel from Peter, and all were baptized (Acts, ch. 10). Lydia, the Philippian businesswoman, when she became a Christian, was baptized together with her household (Acts 16:15), and the Philippian jailer, when he was moved to repentance, at once drew his whole family with him into his act of faith (Acts 16:31-34).

The institution of infant Baptism in the Church is undoubtedly a consequence of this sense of family solidarity. In its origin, Baptism by its nature required that the person should be of an age to make a conscious decision, for it was a symbol of an inner repentance and change of life. But, as the Church spread through a pagan world, a new situation arose when a family head was converted from paganism to faith. Baptism was the mark by which he was claimed for God, an indication that he had left behind him the old life and entered upon the new. But what of his children who were not yet of an age to make a decision for themselves? Must they be left without this precious mark until some indefinite later date? That was unthinkable. They too must be claimed for God and have his mark upon them. They too must share in the new life that had come to the parents. A separation of children from parents at this point would have done violence to the solidarity of the family. Therefore, the children, though infants, were given Baptism as a sign of their admission to the Church.

Infant Baptism has meaning only where parents take seriously their own relation to Christ and to the Church and their Christian function as ministers of God to their own children. They promise " to bring them up in the nurture and admonition of the Lord " and to teach them the truths and duties of the Christian faith. Unfaithfulness in this ministry is a breaking of vows made solemnly before God and is of a gravity equal to the offense of a minister of the Church when he deliberately disregards his ordination vows. Can sacred vows be flouted with impunity? Let men and women lose their respect for their marriage vows and the consequences are disastrous. Let Christian ministers begin to sit lightly to their ordination vows and the whole ministry falls into disorder. And yet the Baptismal vows are regarded widely as a mere formality in a name-giving ceremony, and only too often the parents never give a second thought to what they promised. Abdication by parents of their function as ministers of faith within the home is unfaithfulness to the vows they made before God when they brought their children to be baptized.

Both the solidarity of the family and the importance of the parents' ministry will be better understood if we go back a stage and consider the nature of Christian marriage by which the home comes into being. The marriage ceremony usually begins with the words: " Except the Lord build the house, they labor in vain that build it," which, freely translated, means, " Except God make this marriage and this home, these two people are helpless to reach the goal of their desire." Christian marriage is a miracle, for it is no less than the union of two persons into one person. " They twain shall become one flesh," that is, one person. Marriage that is merely a partnership, merely a sharing of some things in life while each partner retains complete independence, is not Christian but pagan. Marriage without union of persons may have in it a wealth of affection, but at the center, where there should be an indissoluble oneness, there is a dividedness. How can there be a union of persons when it is the nature of human beings to be self-centered and to assert stubbornly the sovereignty of the self? We have to say that where self remains supreme, union with another person is an impossibility. Only where the self has been utterly humbled before God and has been thrust from the place of rule at the center, that God may take his rightful place as sovereign, can there be real community with any other person. For there to be a union of two persons of the completeness that is promised in Christian marriage, both must have found the center of life in God, so that he is the deepest bond of union between them. The humbling of the self and the centering of life in God is the work of Jesus Christ in the human soul. Christian marriage, therefore, in its very nature must be rooted in the Christian faith, and the union, which is God's gracious work in two souls, must constantly be nourished from its original source. In their common worship of God, man and wife are bound ever more closely to each other, and obstacles to their union are cleared out of the way.

As children come, they enter into this circle, sharing in its life, and by their presence strengthening and enriching it. The entire relationship is transformed by the coming of the child, because the child is not a unit added on the outside, but a third person within the unity of the family. To keep the child on the outside, as sometimes happens, is to rob him of the warm living spiritual context of his life, even though he may seem to be provided with all things necessary and to be under the watchful care of responsible parents. They are sharing with him everything that they have, except that which is most necessary — themselves. They will not take the time or pay the spiritual cost of giving *themselves* to their children. And to give themselves would mean to share life with their children on those deeper levels where the questions of faith are inescapable. Thus, it appears that the abdication by the parent of his Christian function and the ignoring of the Christian faith in the home, sets in question actually the Christian character of the home and of the marriage. It is not the loss merely of a single function by the home, but the loss of the divine order of the home. The home is becoming something other than, in the order of his creation, God intended it to be.

The family was founded by God as the basic unit of all human society. The union of man and wife is of an intimacy that goes far beyond all other relationships in its strength and depth, and cannot be shared without being destroyed. That intimacy brings two persons so close to each other that it intensifies the possibility both of joy and of pain. The problems of man's life with man and consequently also of his relationship with God are forced out into the open where they have to be faced as nowhere else. In the home, men and women have to find a solution to the problem of community or be destroyed. And where the home becomes a community, it not only gives to the individuals within it a security and a rocklike basis for their entire living, but lends to the larger social group a greater measure of stability. The decay of the home is a serious matter for any society, for it means the loss by individuals of the primary social context of their lives, and of a very essential security, and also the loss to society as a whole of the stabilizing and enriching influence of the individual families. Even more serious, however, is the loss to the growing children of the warm, intimate family situation in which, with confidence and naturalness, they can find their way to a solution of many of the most important questions of existence. God's order for the home has in it health for man and wife in their relationships with each other, health for growing children, and health for the community at large. It is not hard to see the beneficence of God's plan in making the family the basic unit of human society.

THE LOSS OF THE DIVINE ORDER

The loss, by the Christian home, of its divine order has serious consequences. First to feel the effects are the parents themselves. The status of the parent is no longer the same when the uniquely Christian function is gone. A very clear indication of this change of status is the loss of authority. One hears parents complaining on every side that their children do not respect their parental authority as they ought. " We have done everything for them that a parent can do," they say. " We have given them the best in food and clothing and housing and schooling. We have taken them to church and have sent them to church school." But they do not go on to say that they have been ministers of faith to these children within the home. They expect all the rest to be sufficient without this last.

The only authority that is ultimately effective in the home is spiritual, and requires a minimum of external force. There is always in the background, of course, the possibility of external compulsion, which is based upon the fact that the parent is stronger than the child, that the parent holds the pocketbook and the keys of the house — and the keys of the car. But this kind of authority is essentially impersonal and does not get very far, even with younger children. If it is constantly relied on, it soon creates a reaction of stubborn rebellion and the home is rent by an unending struggle between unyielding contradictory wills. Only the authority of wisdom and love, of truth and justice, operating in the parent, can break through this impasse. What is needed is a consciousness on the part of the child that the parent is not trying arbitrarily to force his will upon him, but, rather, is concerned that each of them may find the solution of his problems that is right, and that together they may discover and fulfill God's will for them. It is when the child is forced by the parent's attitude to look beyond the parent to the God whom the parent unashamedly serves that the deepest respect for the parent's authority is generated. The perspective of all things in the home is changed when the home has its center, not in itself, but in God. Therefore, it is unrealistic for parents to expect to have the authority of Christian parents if they have abandoned the essential functions of Christian parents.

A second consequence is for the child. The child is robbed of what should be the strongest support of his spiritual life. He grows up in a spiritual vacuum. The questions that inwardly he knows are more important than any others in life are ignored in his home. The people to whom he is most deeply attached, who are examples to him of what life can be, seem to him to pass through six days a week without any thought of God. Can we ourselves remember what it was like to be twelve years old? We were coming awake first to one aspect and then another of our existence and of the world about us; we were probing cautiously the mysteries of ourselves and the universe. The dimensions of things, both outwardly and inwardly, were so vast that they were frightening. But our greatest difficulty was that all these mysteries and problems of existence were bottled up inside us, for we could not easily speak of such things to anyone else. What a difference it makes at this stage in a child's life whether or not the home in which he lives is the kind in which all life's problems and difficulties, religious or otherwise, can be discussed freely and frankly! To be able to express a gnawing doubt without shocking anyone, and with the assurance that someone will try to understand, may again and again have a decisive effect upon the child's development. To grow up in an atmosphere where questions relating to the Christian faith are considered important and are taken seriously — this should be the child's heritage. But when this is not so, when the exclusion of religion from discussion is such that to say the word " God " would cause embarrassment, then the growing child's tremendous questions about life are sealed within the mind, perhaps to fester there and cause great unhappiness.

A third consequence is for the home itself. There is concern everywhere about the instability of the home in our time. So many families crack under the strains of modern life and crumble, leaving ugly scars upon those involved, and particularly upon the young. If these families were outside the Christian faith, we would sorrow at the tragedy of their dissolution, but we would not be puzzled, for partnerships are always in danger of dissolution if either partner begins to find the relationship unprofitable or difficult. But so often they are the homes of professing Christians that have either cracked or are in an unstable and unhappy condition. Has it occurred to us, however, to trace a causal connection between the abdication of his Christian function by the parent and the instability of the home? The divine order for the home is that it should be a seedbed of faith, that in its intimacy the environment should be created in which human beings can best grow up in the knowledge and love of God. Abandon that divine order and its surest fundation has been pulled out from under the home. Its life has been condemned to superficiality. It has lost out of itself those elements which alone enable it to meet the deeper needs of human life and to touch those levels of existence on which true reverence and thankfulness are awakened.

What is at stake, then, is not just the encouragement of parents to do a little religious teaching in the home, but something far more crucial — the recovery of the divine order for the home. Too long already we have consented to an abandonment of the divine order, and have been suffering the consequences of that abandonment in impoverishment and confusion of life. A return to the divine order would be the first step in a revolution that could have far-reaching effects, not only upon the life of the church, but also upon the life of the community at large. The family is the primary cell both in the church and in the community, and what happens there eventually bears its fruits for good or for ill in the larger spheres.

In most churches there has been a sharpened awareness of the importance of the home during the past ten years. Magazines have been launched for the instruction and awakening of parents. Some curriculums have built the home into their basic structure and have given parents specific tasks. The Ligon Plan has demonstrated how far parents can be drawn into participation when the trouble is taken to give them a definite part in the program and to train them carefully to do what is asked of them. Many congregations have found it possible to have regular consultations between the parents and the teachers of the church school.

One of the significant discoveries where parents have been awakened to their educational responsibility is that they become keenly aware of their own inadequacies and begin to make more use of their opportunities for gaining a better understanding of their faith. It is when a person undertakes to teach that he learns how little he himself knows, and many things that he has taken for granted must be carefully re-examined. Thus, a recovery of the true Christian order in the home is likely to have as one result the sparking of an adult education movement that could reach very large proportions.

It is well for anyone who attempts to lay hold upon this problem to proceed with due caution. Many parents are so completely on the outside so far as Christian education is concerned that they are easily frightened. They fear that they will be placed in a situation with their own children that will be highly embarrassing to them. A man who has never prayed aloud in the presence of others may so dread having to do it that he would never knowingly enter a meeting where he might be asked to pray. Therefore, they need to be given assurance that they are not going to be pushed into doing things they do not want to do. They must be allowed, with intelligent guidance, to find their own way into a more coherent Christian relationship with their children. Above all, they must learn to pray in their own hearts for their children and for the graces and gifts that will enable them, in a perfectly natural way, to let their Christian faith be manifest and find its rightful place in the life of the home.

10

THE CHURCH AND PUBLIC EDUCATION

THUS far, we have been considering an education that lies wholly within the scope and under the authority of the Church. What is made of it depends upon the Church alone. We turn now to an area of education that lies outside the Church and does not come directly under its authority, the education that is given in publicly operated schools. This area must always be of great concern to the Church, for the Church's members, as they grow to manhood and womanhood, spend a large portion of their time under the shaping influence of these schools. For each hour that they spend in a church school, they usually spend at least twenty hours in a public school. One must remember also the unusual authority that the school and the schoolteacher have over children's minds. Any parent who has tried to correct at home an impression made on his child's mind at school will be prepared to testify to the force of that authority. Thus, if the school and the Church are moving in contrary directions in their education of the child, it is a serious matter for all concerned. It is unhappy for the child and most confusing to find that what he learns in the one school does not agree with what he learns in the other. It is alarming for the Church if, in any degree, education in the public schools is conditioning the mind of youth to resist the Church's teaching. And it is disturbing to the responsible educator if in any section of the community, and particularly the Christian section from which he draws his major support, he sees a growing distrust of public education.

THE THREAT TO CHRISTIANITY

It is essential at the very beginning to state bluntly that this area is one of mounting tensions today. Churchmen are apprehensive that public education is moving in a direction that is likely to lead to an increasing alienation of the mind of our age from the Christian faith. In 1946, C. C. Morrison said in *The Christian Century:* " The fact must now be faced that Protestantism has been losing the mentality of one generation after another of its own youth to a powerfully implemented system of education, whose end product will be a national community in which Protestantism has, if any place at all, only a marginal or survival position." That may seem to be a rather hysterical and exaggerated statement of the case. Few of the teachers in our schools with whom we come in contact have the appearance of exterminators of Protestant Christianity. Many of them are members of our Churches. Most of them, whether definitely Christian or not, are friendly toward any churchman who interests himself in education. But, if you go behind the front row of educators to the philosophers of education who dominate the scene today, the picture is very different. Under the influence of John Dewey in particular, the field of education has been invaded by a type of Humanism that not only regards Christianity and all other historical religions as antiquated superstitions from the past, but is confident that in Humanism modern man finds his only intelligent approach to reality. Many representatives of this school have actually a crusading zeal to deliver mankind from its " superstitions " into the glorious freedom of the completely rational life.

This Humanism can be found at three different levels. First, it is plainly to be seen in philosophers of education such as John Dewey, Boyd H. Bode, and others of similar quality. These are men of such an intellectual stature that they recognize clearly what is involved in their philosophy. If what they believe is true, then Christianity is untrue. They do not shrink from stating their position in all its rigor. They place it in the open for all to see and to consider. There is no concealment.

The second level, however, is that of popularizers of education, such as H. A. Overstreet, whose book *The Mature Mind* has had a wide sale. Here the essential philosophy is the same, but one does not find the same integrity of mind or the same courage that are evident in Dewey and Bode. Either in the confusion of ignorance or in order to gain a wider acceptance for his teaching, Overstreet rep-

resents it as *Christian* teaching. He names Jesus as the finest example
in all history of his " mature man," and the reader has to look very
carefully to discover that by Jesus he does *not* mean the Jesus of
the Gospels who was the Messiah of Israel, the Son of God and the
Saviour of mankind, but a carefully reconstructed Jesus who turns
out to be none other than the ideal Humanist. Toward the close of
Overstreet's book, one finds him almost hysterically angry at the
suggestion that man is a sinner, needing to be redeemed. That assertion he repudiates as an insult to the dignity of man. One must be
more sympathetic to Overstreet in his confusion when one hears a
prominent New York clergyman pronounce the book a fine Christian volume. A church manifesting such flagrant doctrinal blindness dare not be too severe with the befuddlement of the modern
sophist. But we may at least be pardoned for stating categorically
that Overstreet's mature man is not a Christian.

The third level is that of the teacher in the local school who is not
likely to be well-versed in philosophical distinctions, but has been
influenced in his thinking by both the Church and the leading educational philosophies. He wants to be a Christian, but he wants also
to be a self-respecting educator. He may be inclined to welcome a
book such as that of Overstreet which seems to him to reconcile the
two.

An incident in a local church will illustrate the situation. In the
youth department of the church school, the classes were taught by
high school teachers. A unit of seven lessons in the curriculum dealt
with the subject " Christ and Humanism." The purpose of the
lessons was to show young people as definitely as possible the difference between the Christian faith and the Humanist faith, which is
so widespread in America today. In one lesson a comparison was
made between quotations from Dale Carnegie's *How to Win
Friends and Influence People* and quotations from the teachings of
Jesus. In another lesson the so-called religion of the scientist was set
alongside the Christian understanding of the world and the points
of difference marked and explained. But the teachers in a body refused to teach the course. They complained to the director of Christian education that they would need to have had a course in a theological seminary to understand and teach the lessons. The director

complained in turn to the editor who had produced the course that it was folly to give teachers of youth tasks that were completely beyond them. But when the editor and director examined the course in detail, they found that abundant help had been given both for understanding and for teaching the lessons. Eventually the real difficulty came to light when it was discovered that the teachers concerned could not themselves see any valid distinction or contradiction between Christianity and Humanism. To them, Dale Carnegie and Jesus Christ were good companions. Moreover, in their local church, no one had ever undertaken to show them the distinction between the two. In their minds, Christianity and Humanism were inextricably intermingled. These teachers had grown up in the Church, but they had also grown up into a Humanist approach to life.

That is the form in which Humanism most often reaches the local situation, a form that is actually far more difficult to deal with than the primary or pure form in which it is found in Dewey or Bode. And it is this permeation of the educational scene by a Humanist philosophy in a concealed form that is alarming, and ought to be alarming, to Christian churchmen.

THE FEARS OF EDUCATORS

There is another side to the picture. The Church is apprehensive about what is happening in education, but equally the educators are apprehensive at any advance or interference of the Church in the field of public education. The fear is that it may debauch education in the interests of its own propaganda. There have been periods in history when education, under the rigid control of the Church, has been held in a narrow strait jacket and prevented from making advances that would be in the interests of the pupils. In the United States there is no possibility whatsoever of the Protestant Church's trying to control public education. The Protestant Church, in its various denominations, has no means of exercising such a control, and moreover, Protestants in general are ready to support the long-standing tradition of public education being under the direction of the State. Educators are jealous of the freedom that this order provides for them and resent even the slightest move by the Church that modifies it in any way. The school, they say, in order to be the school for all without discrimination, for Christians and non-Christians alike, must be kept in total isolation from the Church.

This point of view received substantial support from the decision of the Supreme Court in the McCallum case in Champaign, Ill. An atheist mother protested to the courts than an injustice was being done her son by the existence of a released time program in the Champaign schools in which children of various religious groups were released from school for an hour each week for religious instruction. The decree of the court was that co-operation of the schools to secure or aid religious teaching of any kind was contrary to the Constitution of the nation, and the judges used the phrase, " A complete wall of separation between Church and State." In actuality, the wall is breached in our schools at thousands of points, for there are still extensive programs of religious teaching being carried on in various forms with the co-operation of the school authorities. But we have had at least a spectacular instance of resistance on the part of the community to any infiltration of the public education system with Christian teaching, and quite a number of books have appeared, arguing both for and against the validity of the Supreme Court's decision.

The Larger Setting of the Problem

If we are to see the problem under consideration with clearness, however, we must put it in a larger setting. The relations between the Church and public education cannot be rightly understood except in the context of the larger and more comprehensive problem of the relations between Christianity and culture. Just as the Church is the unique representative of Christianity in the community, so must the school be recognized as the unique representative of culture. By culture is to be understood the whole network of social, intellectual, economic, political, and artistic realities that make up our life. Some might prefer to call it civilization. However we describe it, there is a body of knowledge and experience that must be passed on from one generation to the other and added to by each new generation, a knowledge and experience that have to do with solving the problems of our daily existence. There are material problems for which we require some background in mathematics and science. There are economic and political problems in which we shall be hopelessly at sea unless we know our history and our social sciences. Literature, art, and music give expression to what is within man in such a way that, through them, he widens the borders of his own being and explores the whole world of human experience. For the furtherance of these cultural purposes, the community provides not only grade schools and high schools but colleges, universities, schools of music and art, technical schools, museums, and various other institutions. We must also recognize that, in the shaping of the culture of a time such as ours, newspapers, magazines, radio, television, and motion pictures have a vastly greater influence than schools and universities. Nevertheless, the school is the place in the community where the cultural problem comes to a focus and a conscious effort is made to determine in what direction our culture should develop. The problem of culture is the problem of the shaping of all those complex forces that make up the day-by-day life of man. The interest of education is not just the communication of information on a number of subjects or the training of the powers of the mind, but rather the preservation and enrichment and deepening of the cultural heritage of the community.

Here is the point, however, where the Christian must speak up. It is possible for human culture to take a number of variant forms, some of them much more sympathetic to the Christian faith than others. It is possible for human culture to take a form that is in absolute contradiction to the Christian faith. Behind every culture, determining the direction of its development, are certain principles, certain conceptions of the world and man and of what matters most in human life. These principles may be Christian or non-Christian or anti-Christian, or they may be a confusion of all three. But it is certainly a matter of the greatest importance to the Church and to Christians what principles underlie the culture of their time.

In the Roman world, which for centuries had been shaped in its inner and outer life by Greek thought, a magnificent unified structure had evolved, which in all its aspects was the expression of the Greek view of life. C. N. Cochrane, in his *Christianity and Classical Culture*, one of the theological classics of this century, shows in the most intricate detail how the Greek conception of God, of man, and of the world led inevitably to the forms of political, social, economic, intellectual, and moral life that were securely established in the Empire in the early years of the Christian Era. He then shows how the Christian doctrine of God, of man, and of the world, but particularly the whole understanding of reality that is embodied in the doctrine of the Trinity, resulted in a wholly new approach to the problems of everyday life and demanded a new kind of culture. Therefore, the growth of the Christian movement in the Empire was not just the growth of a new religion, but was soon perceived to be the emergence of a total structure of life which challenged the validity of the existing cultural forms. This was what accounted for the antagonism of many of the most civilized and intelligent men in the Empire to the seemingly insignificant Christian Church. That Church's faith was a threat to the existence of their world. But equally true was it that the culture of the Empire was a constant threat to the existence of the Church. The Church was under pressure for centuries to compromise with Greek culture and so make itself more at home in the world. But whenever it compromised, it betrayed its own gospel and began to lose the very reason for its own existence.

Richard Niebuhr has performed a great service in the clarifying of this problem in his book *Christ and Culture*. He lets us see that this is no new problem that has suddenly arisen for us, but rather that it is as old as the Church itself. The Church in every age has had to wrestle with the problem of its relation to the culture of its time. Not just one, but a variety of solutions have been proposed in the course of history. Sometimes Christians have made a sharp division between Christianity and culture as though the two could be kept in complete isolation. Thus, a man tries to live in two separate compartments, with his culture in the one and his religion in the other. That is the relationship which the Supreme Court's decision demands. A complete wall of separation between Church and State, as interpreted by them, would mean a complete wall of separation between religion and culture. Some churches have traditionally favored this order, regarding the whole realm of culture as worldly and therefore evil, and counseling for the Christian a life of withdrawal from the world. But this is a denial of the sovereignty of God over the whole of his creation and of the Lordship of Christ over all things in man's life. The claim that God makes upon us is a totalitarian claim. No area of our existence can be kept separate from his rule without remaining in darkness and under the power of evil. Christ is not the redeemer of a disembodied soul but of the whole man in every aspect of his daily life. For that reason the Christian must reject any attempt to divide his life into separate compartments, as though there were portions of it in which he would be free to obey some other command than the command of Jesus Christ and in which he should look for his salvation to some other source than the gospel.

Another possible relationship between Christianity and culture is that of the early centuries of the Church when the Church had to live in defiance of the dominant culture of the time. That is a painful situation for the Christian, for it means that, in order to become a Christian, he has to break with the whole familiar order of life in which he has grown up. His culture and his religion are at war with each other and he has to choose between the two. We glory in the heroic faith of the Christian in ancient times who faced that conflict, and of the Christians who have found themselves in the same state of tension in Nazi and Communist civilizations in the modern world. But we are much slower to recognize elements of the same situation in our American world. We know that Christians in China and Russia must live in sharp and painful tension with the existing culture, but we do not know that Christians in America must also live in an atmosphere of tension.

No error is more widespread today than that of assuming that *our* civilization, *our* culture, is Christian. It has Christian elements in it, because the Christian faith has been exerting a powerful influence upon it for centuries, but in many, many aspects of its life our culture is not Christian at all, but is pagan. This is true, not only of America, but of the whole of our Western civilization. Sir Richard Livingstone, writing some years ago concerning the sources of our Western culture, pointed out that it was built far more on a Greek foundation than upon a Christian one. He claimed that it was over 80 per cent Greek. A striking feature of C. N. Cochrane's portrayal of civilization in the Roman Empire before Christianity made any serious inroads upon it is that at almost every step we feel ourselves to be in some strange way not in Rome but in the contemporary scene, looking out upon Western civilization in the twentieth century. We have assumed too lightly that our civilization is Christian, and what is happening now, both in the educational sphere and elsewhere, is that we are being shocked awake to the realization that the culture in which we have our daily life is Christian in only a very small degree and that non-Christian and even anti-Christian forces predominate in wide aspects of our culture.

Here is the background, then, against which we must set the problem of the church and public education. The school is merely one aspect of a much larger picture, and what is happening in the school is the consequence of much larger and farther reaching developments in the whole of our culture. Perhaps John Dewey and his colleagues are performing a greater service for us than we know by puncturing our delusion that our culture is Christian and standing forth, frankly and honestly, as representatives and prophets of a non-Christian culture. They are more honest and more realistic, and therefore much less dangerous, than sentimental Christians who keep identifying Christianity with American civilization and refusing to recognize the definitely non-Christian and even anti-Christian character of the world in which we live.

Nothing is commoner today than the identification of Christianity with the "American way of life." We hear men calling for a great crusade by the church schools to defend the American way of life against Communism. The American way of life is American civilization, just as the Roman way of life was Roman civilization, and the German way of life was German civilization. It is not hard for us, looking back across the centuries, to see the distinction between the highest forms of Roman culture and Christianity, or, looking across the ocean, to recognize the difference between German *Kultur* and Christianity. But when it is our own nation, to which we are passionately devoted, and our own society, in which we have grown from infancy, and our own culture, in which we are involved in a thousand ways, it is much more difficult for us to grasp the possibility that there may be important elements in it that are in radical contradiction to the Christian faith. Pride and national loyalty makes us tend to assume the Christian character of our particular " way of life." It is at this point that the influence of men such as Dewey may be most salutary, forcing us to recognize that, for some of the clearest-minded of our citizens, our culture is definitely other than Christian in its essential character. The problem we have on our hands begins now to appear in its full magnitude. It is not confined to the schools. It is to be met on every hand, for a culture is all-pervasive, invading our homes and our churches without asking our leave, creating the atmosphere of political and social life, determining how we deal with each other in business, and constantly seeping into the inmost recesses of our souls.

THE CHRISTIAN AND THE HUMANIST ELEMENTS IN EDUCATION

It would be unfortunate if a polemic against a Humanist philosophy of education were to create the impression that a really Christian school would turn its back upon all that is non-Christian and would give its attention only to those aspects of culture that support or can be built into a Christian point of view. The school must take account of our entire cultural heritage if it is to perform its rightful service to the community. If it ignores the Christian heritage, then it falsifies the picture of our culture and it falsifies history and gives our youth a bleeding segment of life rather than life as it is. But, equally true, it cannot ignore the non-Christian elements in our heritage without falsifying the picture. Plato is one of the creators of our world and his influence extends widely through our culture. It is well for the Christian to know what Plato's religion was, and to be able to recognize the difference between it and the Christian faith. But also he needs the contribution that Plato can make to his thinking, and he can recognize in it a very real gift of God. God's decisive revelation of himself to man is through Israel, and through Him who is born of Israel's stock, but God has been at work in all his creation and his hand can be seen far beyond Israel. Greece has its place, and it should be a place of high honor, in God's providence for man. Plato was not wrong in his conviction that his passion for truth had its source in God. We must be open to receive God's good gifts to us, not only through Greece, but from countless other sources. They have come into our culture, and they continue to come as the channels are kept open. So also in the present day we are indebted to non-Christians for countless advances in our knowledge. We do not ask whether or not the scientist or the scholar is a Christian but only whether or not what he has to say is true. The Christian's conviction is that all truth is of God.

What dare not happen, however, is that one should go on from this statement to an attempt to harmonize and unite the Christian and the non-Christian forces in culture into an eclectic religion. Syntheses of this kind have been attempted over and over by Christians and invariably result in a smudging of distinctions to the disadvantage of both elements. We get a Platonized Christianity which is no longer Christianity or a Christianized Plato who is no longer Plato. We must let Jesus Christ be Jesus Christ, and Plato Plato, and Confucius Confucius. We must let each speak in his own way. Our cultural responsibility is to listen to each in turn and to learn from them what they have to teach us. But our Christian responsibility is different. It does not ask of us a partisan loyalty to Jesus Christ and a corresponding antipathy to all others, but only that we recognize the impossibility of having more than one Lord over us, and that we make up our minds whether or not Jesus Christ is Lord of our life. To be a Christian is to have him as Lord and so to be unable to fall into a vague, impersonal religion that tries to give allegiance to the variegated truths of all religions and all cultures. But when he is Lord, he shows himself Lord far beyond Israel and the Church and opens doors for us into riches of life in a thousand different quarters. Even the treasures of the unbelieving Gentiles he makes his own and shares them with us.

The Policy of the Church

It is this vast problem of Christianity and culture that confronts us when we begin to take seriously the question of the Church's relation to public education. It is so vast that it is trifling for the Church to concentrate all its energies upon trying merely to get a little Bible teaching into the public schools. An hour of Bible each week, taught in isolation from all other subjects, is not likely to do very much for the Christianization of our culture. It is worth striving for and can contribute in the course of years to the solution of the problem. But it is utter folly for the Church to let its chief interest in public education center upon that hour of Bible teaching, or, where it has provided such an hour, for it to sit back complacently as though it had now contributed the proper Christian element to education. The Church's concern must be with the total character of education and of the culture of which the educational institutions are merely the expression.

We see also what folly it is for the Church, when it discovers non-Christian Humanists among the educators of our time, to become hysterical and exhaust its educational concern in shouting about the godlessness of our public education. It would be much more in order for the Church, before it speaks too loudly, to show that it understands the problem and to produce a Christian philosophy of education as thorough and as practical as that which has been produced by the Humanists. The fact is that the Church has not taken its cultural responsibility with sufficient seriousness to be able to speak as convincingly in this realm as it ought. A Christian education in colleges and universities has all too often been conceived as merely Humanist education with a Bible course added and with compulsory attendance at chapel.

The proposal has sometimes been made, that, since the public schools have in such a measure become propagators of a non-Christian Humanist philosophy of life, the Protestant Church should establish parochial schools over which it would have complete control. But what guarantee is there that the teachers in these parochial schools would be representatives of a thoroughly Christian culture? As we have already seen, a man may be a member of the Church and an earnest Christian and yet unconsciously determined in his culture, not by the Christian faith, but by the Humanist environment in which he has grown up. Also, can a Protestant with a Christian conscience withdraw from his missionary responsibility in the community? Can he, in order to safeguard the souls of children of church families, abandon the public schools and all the children in them to whatever non-Christian interests care to take control of them? Surely that would be a counsel of despair both for the nation and for the Church.

Behind the parochial school lies a third conception of the relationship between Christianity and culture, that the Church should secure a Christian culture by taking the educational institutions of the community directly under its control. If we are to understand why the Roman Catholic Church and others have favored this solution, we must grasp the fact that education, because it deals with the whole man, is inevitably involved in religious presuppositions. An absolute separation of education and religious principles of some kind is an impossibility. Education, by its very nature, demands a religious foundation. The educator in so far as he is a good educator, concerned not just to transmit information but to shape the lives of persons, is forced to ask ultimate questions about the meaning of life. He has in his hands the molding of lives, but in what direction is he to mold them? He must give some answer to the question, What is the rightful nature of man?, and the answer he gives will determine the character of his influence. He must grapple with the meaning of the world about which he is teaching, and, if he does so, he is confronted by the question of the ultimate reality, God. All education, in so far as it goes beyond the technical and is truly cultural, has a religious significance and is based on theological presuppositions, whether they are acknowledged or not. An untheological educator is an impossibility. It has never yet been seen in the world, nor will it ever be seen.

It is in recognition of this that the Roman Catholic Church has always insisted upon controlling the schools in which its children are educated. Its aim is not, as people think, merely to keep the children constantly under the Church's authority. Rather, it is to prevent a dangerous split in the very souls of its people between their faith and their culture. If they are educated in a culture that proceeds on the basis of a theology that is in contradiction to the theology they are taught by their Church, they will suffer from a painful confusion, even though they are not able of themselves to perceive the contradiction, and the more they absorb of the alien culture, the more likely they will be to turn against their Church. Therefore, the Roman Catholic Church tries to provide for all its children from their earliest years a cultural situation that will be in fullest harmony with the principles and practices of the Church. The important thing in their parochial schools is not the unlimited opportunity for teaching religion but rather the character that is given to all the other subjects of study. Thomas J. Quigley, superintendent of Roman Catholic schools in Pittsburgh, in an article in *Religious Education* magazine in 1944, told how, in the early days of parochial schools in America, the same textbooks were used as in other schools, with a course in religion merely as an appendix to the whole. But this was recognized as contrary to the traditional Roman Catholic philosophy of education. They could not be satisfied until they had a curriculum with " courses in the natural sciences, the social sciences, citizenship, and health, all thoroughly grounded in the Roman Catholic philosophy of life, the Roman Catholic interpretation of the relationship between God, the individual, and society, and all closely correlated with the principles of Catholic religion." " The music and art courses in the schools have also been brought into line, and valuable use is being made of church art and liturgical music in the classroom. Series of elementary school readers have been published through which religious doctrine and religious ideals are introduced to the child in the primary grades and are made to keep pace with his maturing personality."

There may be a suspicion in our minds that this is an interjecting of religion into subjects with which it has nothing to do, and therefore we may not be willing to regard it as conclusive proof of the religious involvement of all education. But perhaps we shall be more impressed with the soundness of Roman Catholic educational thinking when he have heard several witnesses who come from the opposite extreme in education. Ironic as it may seem, John Dewey, who is regarded as the very fountainhead of modern secularized education, is forced by the inner logic of his conception of education into assertions that are basically theological in character. Education for him is a redemptive process. It is the agency through which society may be brought eventually to its fulfillment. Education is merely a speeding up of the process by which a society constantly criticizes and evaluates its experience, thereby leaving behind its inadequacies and gaining for itself a fuller life. The nature of the education is determined by the nature of the goal which society has before it. But when he attempts to describe this goal and what man is meant to be, Dewey is fully conscious that he is raising ultimate questions and that the answers he gives to them are religious answers. It is this awareness that led him, a few years ago, to write a little book, *A Common Faith*, in which he confesses his own religious faith and proposes it as a possible religion for intelligent men the world over. It is a very naïve document theologically, but one that nevertheless shows how Dewey, in spite of his antagonism to existing historical religions, was convinced that a stable culture must rest upon a religious foundation, and that few of the elements in human life that he valued most would have power to survive without the support and encouragement of a religious interpretation of reality.

Boyd H. Bode, in a very able book published in 1940, *How We Learn*, finds himself stumbling onto theological questions in the final stages of his discussion. Since education has the task of reshaping the life of man, ethical standards are of paramount importance. But these standards, he insists, must be drawn by the man of today out of his immediate experiences of life. The criterion, for there must be a criterion, is what will best serve the strengthening and enrichment of democratic society. For Bode, as for Dewey, democracy is both religion and church. Democracy is the authority that must not be questioned. Here is an interesting quotation. " Democracy as a way of life," says Bode, " is committed to the proposition that man must place sole reliance on his unaided intelligence both for the discovery of methods for the exercise of control over his material and social environment and for construction of the ends to be achieved." In simpler terms, in a democratic society the sovereignty of man's reason must alone be recognized in religion and ethics. Reason is man's only dependable God. In allegiance to this principle, Bode rejects all forms of religion that find the origin and basis of ethics in the supernatural. The passion with which he rejects them arises from the fact that, for him, the system of education that he has developed is to all intents and purposes a redemptive religion. It is the means, and he does not hesitate to claim that it is the *only* means, by which human life can be brought to its fulfillment. What have we here except a dogmatic Humanist religion which already has begun to assert, in the most exclusive spirit, that it is for man the only way of salvation? One cannot refrain from venturing the suggestion that if there should ever develop a totalitarian democracy in America — and let us remember what Emil Brunner warned us long ago, that a totalitarian democracy is possible — and if this totalitarian democracy desired a religion to support it more wholeheartedly than any form of the Christian religion ever could, it would find an authoritative, scientific, democratic religion ready-made for it in the books of our leading Humanist educators. They are the prophets of an American democratic Humanist civilization, liberated from the imprisoning fetters of Christianity.

The point, however, that I want to drive home is that, wherever education is taken seriously, the educator finds himself inevitably asking ultimate questions about the nature and destiny of man and about the meaning of the world in which he lives. He is forced by the nature of his work to be in some measure a theologian. He cannot escape from it. He may be consciously and responsibly a theologian, or he may take over his basic conceptions ready-made from both Christian and non-Christian sources without being conscious of the contradictions in them; but a religiously neutral education is an impossibility.

Considered in this light, the judgment of the Supreme Court in the McCallum case must be interpreted merely as a restraint of organized churches from having control of any part of public education, and not as a demand for complete separation of religion and education. The prophet of a Humanist religion is free to propagate his faith to his heart's content in the public education system. But so also is the Christian free to bear witness to the cultural implications of the Christian faith. Just as we do not ask the Humanist to be anything other than a Humanist, so also the Christian educator must know that he is free to be a Christian and need not conceal in any way his Christian convictions as he discharges his educational responsibility. This does not mean that the Christian teacher should try to turn the school into a church and to use his point of vantage to evangelize the pupils. That would be folly and would rightly be prohibited by the authorities. His task is to be a Christian *educator,* to do the work of education with thoroughness and effectiveness upon the basis of his Christian convictions and his Christian understanding of man and the world. What he does with students outside the school as they consult him with their personal problems is his own concern. The community has no right to silence his Christian witness, or to silence the Humanist's Humanist witness.

The Church's first task, then, is to produce Christian educators, men and women who are active, intelligent Christian disciples, and at the same time competent in the field of education, who can command respect not only by the integrity of their faith but also by the high quality of their educational workmanship. We ought not to pin our hopes of influencing education upon one hour a week of Bible teaching, but rather, upon twenty-five hours a week of cultural activity based upon and impregnated with Christian principles. If Humanism has gained the upper hand in many of our schools and among philosophers of education, then one must ask, What have fifty million Christians been doing to let themselves be outthought in this way? The remedy is not to start a futile war on Humanists in education, but to outwork and outthink the Humanists in the educational task.

There is a story told of a Scotsman who brought his son down from the hills to be educated in the town. To the dominie in charge of the school, he confided that, if the lad found grace, he hoped to make a minister of him. " And what if he doesn't find grace? " the dominie asked. And the Highlander answered, " Then we'll just have to be content to make a dominie of him." Too often that has been the Church's blind spot toward education. It has failed to see in it a full Christian vocation. And it has failed to work out a Christian philosophy of education that would make clear the implications of the Christian faith for the whole field of culture. If men today feel a sharp cleft between their Christianity and their culture, if the strengthening of their cultural interest often results in their alienation from the Church, the responsibility is in a large measure the Church's because of its tendency to identify religion solely with activities within the Church, with a consequent neglect of the implications of faith for every aspect of human culture. If the culture of our time has increasingly taken a coloration antithetical to the Christian faith, that may well be because those who are carrying cultural responsibilities in the community have not heard from the Church any clear word of guidance in regard to the problems with which they have to deal.

First, then, let the Church set its own house in order, so that within its own gates education in the Christian faith may be of a character that commands respect from educators and theologians alike. It must take both words with complete seriousness — " education " and " Christian." Perhaps then it will have the strength and competence to take a more active part in the field of public education, not attempting to gain direct control of its processes, but taking infinite pains to make clear, point by point, in the culture of our time the implications of the Christian faith for every aspect of the life of man.

CONCLUSION

SUCH, then, is the character of our educational problem, both within the Church and beyond the Church in the community. At every point it has become evident that it is a theological problem. Because education is concerned with the shaping of the whole being of persons, it cannot escape having in it assumptions, whether explicit or implicit, about the nature and destiny of man, assumptions that rest upon a basis that can only be described as faith. If it is not the Christian faith, then it is some other faith. Non-Christian faiths may clothe themselves in highly attractive garments and may claim to be not faiths at all but merely the consequence of a rational examination of all the facts concerning man and the universe. But, strangely, the conclusions show a remarkable resemblance to the assumptions with which the investigator approached his task. Humility and honesty surely demand that Christian and non-Christian alike admit that in their investigations they are incapable of complete objectivity where their own existence is concerned. The antithesis therefore is not between objective educational scientists and biased Christian educators but rather between educators who are committed to a Humanist understanding of the world and man, and educators who are committed to a Christian understanding of the world and man. The one may be equally scientific with the other. Neither can escape from his involvement in a faith and so in a theology.

This theological character of education appears at every level in the Church's program. The stories that are told to four-year-old children will naturally be devoid of formal theological words and expressions but they will have a theological content and will belong in some major theological context. In short, some kind of faith is expressed in them and we should know what it is. If stories for small children embody a view of nature that is essentially pantheistic (which they often have in the past), then we may expect to find elements of pantheism in the minds of those children years later. Sow pantheistic ideas and you must expect to reap a pantheist. Perhaps an even better example is the effect upon the minds of children of interpretations of Jesus that make it very difficult for them to grasp the fact that he was wholly human. Many young people find that it involves a revolution in their thinking to comprehend the New Testament picture of Jesus. The teacher of small children, by a false simplification of the question who Jesus is, or by failing to have seen what it means to assert both the humanity and the divinity of Jesus, may confuse the mind of the child for years to come.

A teacher who refuses to recognize the need for theological understanding and discrimination in the work of teaching is guilty of irresponsibility. He is in a class with the man " who didn't know the gun was loaded." As teachers we are impressing a theology of some kind upon the minds and hearts of our students. We need to know what it is and to be constantly working at the task of finding our own way to a truer and more effective Christian theology. The theological question in Christian education is not to be regarded as having to do only with the foundation of education. It is involved in every part of it, so that we must speak of the theological *character* of education, and as educators we must willingly and gladly take up our task as theologians.

If the arguments of these chapters are sound, they lead to some important practical conclusions. They call for reconsideration of the place of Christian education in the theological curriculum and of the place of basic theological disciplines in the curriculum of schools of education. They raise sharply the question of the unity of the ministry, and the right of those who are teachers rather than preachers to share in the full ministry when they are properly trained. They point to the importance of more thorough training in Bible, history, and doctrine for church school teachers. They call for a recognition by the congregation as a whole of its responsibility for teaching. Above all, they set a new aim for education, one that is significant for a Church that is interested in regaining its evangelizing power. The call we hear is simply the call to be the Church for which Jesus Christ lived and died, a royal priesthood, daring to put itself at his service to be used by him for his conquest of the world.